Why Should I Care?

WILLIAM R. GRIMBOL

Why Should I Care?

HONEST ANSWERS TO THE QUESTIONS THAT TROUBLE TEENS

AUGSBURG Publishing House • Minneapolis

WHY SHOULD I CARE?
Honest Answers to the Questions that Trouble Teens

Library of Congress Cataloging-in-Publication Data

Grimbol, William R., 1950–
Why Should I Care?

Summary: Offers advice, from a Christian point of view, on dealing with a variety of situations that confront teenagers including divorce, peer pressure, suicide, unreliable or abusive parents, and death.
1. Youth—religious life. 2. Youth—Conduct of life. [1. Conduct of life. 2. Christian life]
I. Title.
BV4531.2.G77 1988 248.8'3 88-7503
ISBN 0-8066-2363-2

Manufactured in the U.S.A. APH 10-7176

2 3 4 5 6 7 8 9 0 1 2 3 4 5 6 7 8 9

To the youth of the
Shelter Island Community Youth Center
who have become my personal answer
to the question addressed in this book

Contents

Preface

Being a teenager can be a real roller coaster experience. Some days you feel so high you think you can conquer the world. Other days you're so low that all you can think is, "Who cares?" or "Why bother?" The tough part of being a teenager is that you are encouraged to ignore those down times or never admit when you feel like you've hit bottom. It's hard to act "together" when you feel like you're falling apart. And it's difficult to pretend you have all the answers, when actually all you have is a ton of questions.

Being an adolescent is filled with growing pains, and that means going through some real uphill battles. I thought it might be helpful to share with you a time in my life when I felt trapped in growing pains, a time when my roller coaster felt stuck in a deep valley.

I remember it so clearly, like you would recall a first kiss or a favorite Christmas. The sky was a cool, crisp, spotless blue. The trees were coated in copper and burning with reds and oranges, and the sun was just warm enough to let us be outside without need of coats or jackets. I was leaving an English class, a course on Shakespeare that I was surprised to find myself enjoying, and had decided to go sit for a bit on Old Main Hill. I walked by a touch football game, two major wrestling matches in the leaves, and a swarm of students heading for the cafeteria. Once at the hill, my favorite thinking spot, I suddenly found myself sobbing. I was terrified that anyone would see me crying so hard, so I pretended to be taking a quick nap with my arms folded tightly across my eyes.

I didn't know why I felt the way I did. I was popular—vice president of the student body, getting good grades, and dating regularly. From all outward appearances I was your basic "normal" adolescent. However, what had shattered my "totally together" image on that hill was the sudden recognition that for the last several weeks I had been really feeling down. In fact, quite often I had even wondered what it would be like to just end it all.

As I sat sobbing on Old Main Hill, I was stung by the awareness of just how lonely I felt, how unhappy and insecure. I know now that I didn't really want to die, but I was exhausted with living as a phoney. No matter how it looked to everyone else, I felt as hollow as a Halloween pumpkin, and my carved smile was just as fake. I could not imagine continuing to live feeling so empty and artificial.

Ever since that day on Old Main Hill I have been haunted by the question, What happened to get me so down, so low, that I even considered suicide? I have had to learn how to be more honest with myself, not only about what I am feeling, but who I really am. I have gone through counseling. I have studied. I have prayed. I have discussed. I have listened. I have worked hard to understand what happened to me, and to figure out how to handle the low points in life.

I also have been involved in youth ministry, and I've had thousands of conversations with teens who were just as troubled as I had been and thousands more with young people who may not have been as depressed, but who could understand my feelings, thoughts, and questions. I have come to realize that my experience was not unique . . . and that my questions were really *our* questions.

Recently, I have felt called to write about what happened to me, but more important, about what I have come to realize has also been painfully experienced by so many of you. I share this book with you not as an expert—I don't believe there are any—nor as a magic wand to make the growing pains of being a teenager disappear. I share with you what you have shared with me—your thoughts, your feelings, and, most of all, your questions. I share with you what I have discovered about growing up in a stressful, modern world.

I also choose to share my faith with you, to remind you that you are never alone, and that Jesus Christ is really at your side. With Jesus as a friend and partner, I believe you can enjoy the roller coaster ride of being a teen. I hope you discover as I did, that with Jesus close beside and inside you, you can cope with the growing pains, and even face *your own* most difficult questions. With Jesus, your hope for a brighter tomorrow is not only a real hope, but a sure thing.

Introduction
"WHO AM I?"

These are not, I repeat, *not* the best years of your life. In fact, whoever coined that phrase is probably responsible for the reason so many young people feel it is unacceptable to admit to being sad or down or depressed. Adolescence is a stormy time of life, a time filled with questions, fears, and doubts. It is a period of time when you strangely want to be both unique and a part of the crowd. A key question of adolescence, and a question common to all of you, is, "Who am I?" And this natural and very normal teenage question leads you to ask more disturbing ones:

"What are my needs?"
"What do I really want out of life?"
"What do I believe in?"
"How do I know when I'm in love?"
"What's my purpose in life?"
"Who are my real friends?"
"Why do I get so angry? so hurt? so down?"

Let's face it, being a teenager is a time drenched in questions, and finding the answer to "Who am I?" will take at least a lifetime. To say that adolescence is stormy is an understatement, when you consider the hurricane of questions being asked.

Chris, a high school senior from New York and a member of my youth group, describes these rocky teen times accurately: "I spend almost every day secretly worrying about how I look, how I sound, how I come across, worrying about college and the future and whether I'll have anything good to do this weekend. I try to act 'laid back,' but most of the time I'm really uptight. I feel on the verge of throwing up half the time."

Steve, another senior from the same youth group, offers this description of the trials of being a teen: "I feel stretched in a million directions. I try to be what my parents want, my friends want, what I'm told to be on TV, and I have zero idea of who I am. Zip!"

Part of finding out who you are is discovering who you are away from home. Your need to declare some independence from family often expresses itself in angry explosions:

"I'm not your little kid!"

"I can't wait to get out of this house!"

"Just leave me alone!"

"Quit treating me like a baby!"

"I just don't believe in what you believe in anymore!"

"I'll do it any way I want to!"

Though you may be aware that you can never know who you are until you leave the nest, it is still a frightening thought to ask yourself, "Will I make it on my own?" You may feel like you are caught on a trapeze suspended in mid-air somewhere between home and the thing they call "the real world."

You can't ever answer the question, "Who am I?" unless you are are also willing to find out who other people think you are. The need for friends and romance is a dominant force in adolescence, and it uses up a great deal of your energy. It is fair to say that without friendship and love, there is no possible way to get an accurate portrait of who you are.

It should also be said that "falling in love" is a big fall, and a huge risk. The fall of love is frightening and adds even more swirling questions to the hurricane:

"Will I be loved in return?"

"Will I do it right?" (both emotionally and sexually speaking).

"What if we break up?"

"How can I handle feeling this out of control?"

"Why do I feel so vulnerable?"

Love is a necessary experience of life, but it is also hard work and requires taking a really risky leap of faith.

The question, "Who am I?" is at the core of your emotional world, and serves as the creator of a flock of companion questions. Though these questions make the teen years pretty tough and pretty troubling, most of you will manage to come through the experience in excellent shape. In fact, you will have done something quite valuable—called *maturing*—during your teenage roller coaster ride.

However, over the years since my Old Main Hill breakthrough, I have come to realize that there are some deeper questions, some questions I think are brand new, some questions unique to our American culture, that can at times become overwhelming for you—even life threatening. Such potentially "killing" questions are becoming more and more common, and it seems that teens' ability to cope with them is becoming less and less.

The rest of this book will deal with 10 of these questions, questions that are more complex and even more hurtful than asking, "Who am I?" I don't mean to say that asking these questions is automatically deadly, since that definitely is not the case. Some of you will ask all 10 and never even show any damage. Still, for some of you, for some of your friends, or even for friends you have not met yet, these questions can be brutal. They could even become deadly if they arrive in multiples of two or three or four, or when your faith or spirits are at a record low, or when family or friendship support has vanished.

What about answers, you ask? Well, I will not be offering you questions only. I hope to share 10 faith-centered responses as well. Jesus Christ does not offer some magic solution for all of life's pains and questions, but he is the source of strength to get you through. Jesus won't remove these questions from your world, but he can offer you the courage to live out an answer you can be proud of. I know for myself, my relationship to Jesus Christ was crucial to facing my growing pains, pains caused by questions that I now know last a lifetime.

It is my hope that this book will help you understand the troubling questions teens ask today, as well as offer some clues on how your faith in Jesus can become a significant resource for learning how to handle your own growing pains.

In the United States alone, 500,000 young people attempt suicide every year. As Christians we all have a responsibility to know more about the experience of being a teenager today. You especially need to know more about who you are, so that the more troubling questions of your world and your times cannot defeat you. You may not be part of today's teen suicide problem, but you surely can be part of the solution. Whatever the case, you can *deepen* in your own self-awareness, in your insight into others, in your courage to handle your questions, in your spiritual strength to deal with your growing pains, and in your faith to face the future confidently. This book is about going deeper in life, learning to avoid being shallow or superficial. Depth always begins with digging, and digging means questions. Here we go!

"WHY ME?"

Givens

Some of you may be having a difficult time coping with the *givens* of life. What is a *given?* A given is a fact of life, a characteristic or quality about you, your family, or your world, that you believe will never change, or that will change only if a miracle occurs. Though certain givens can and will change over the course of time, it is your belief that they will go on forever. However, there are many givens that are permanent fixtures of life, and you must either accept them or at least cope with them. Let me give you some examples:

1. An outstanding physical feature, such as a big nose or large ears, or being very tall or real short, or being quite fat or quite skinny.

2. Your I.Q.
3. Athletic coordination.
4. Physical attractiveness or unattractiveness.
5. A physical handicap.
6. A prominent scar.
7. A learning disability.
8. The lack of family financial resources.
9. A parent without an education.
10. A parent without social rank or a so-called prestige profession.

As you can see, givens cover the works—everything from an overbite to a scar, from not having the money to buy designer clothes to being lousy at tumbling. These givens I have mentioned—and you can probably cite a hundred more—may not appear to be worthy of much worry or the cause of much pain, but let me show you how they can become for some of you a "Why Me?" situation.

Stuart

Stuart is a handsome young man, a top student and athlete, and has a personality with great charisma. He came to see me with the complaint, "My world is falling apart." After listening to Stuart for about 20 minutes, it was clear that he was in great emotional pain, and much of his world was indeed collapsing. His grades had fallen. He was constantly irritable with his girlfriend, and he had recently exploded with his parents, calling them "every name in the book." Stuart's problem was that he was losing his hair at age 17, and would probably be bald on top in no more than two years. Sound silly? Well, to Stuart it wasn't.

It was constantly on his mind. "I think I can hear it falling out. It sounds like glass shattering on the floor," he said. For Stuart, the loss of hair at such an early age was a given that was creating pure panic inside—"Why me?"

Ken

Ken was the school's premier athlete. He had won nine letters in three years, and last year was All-State in football and baseball. If he won varsity letters in three sports again—a sure thing—he would be the first person to win 12 letters in the school's history. And if he made All-State a second time, this too would become part of the school's and his athletic legacy.

The summer before his senior year, Ken could feel the pressure mounting, and he was secretly terrified of living up to everyone's extraordinary expectations of him, especially his parents. One morning that summer, Ken went to the school weight room quite early, and while nobody was watching, took a hundred-pound weight and dropped it on his foot. His foot was smashed, and his season was over.

Ken came to me asking, "Why me?" Why did everyone expect so much? Why did he have to be so athletically gifted? Maybe you have always dreamed of having Ken's problems, but for him, it had become a gift with a very high emotional and spiritual price tag.

Denise

Denise was a hard-working, attractive 10th grader. She got very respectable grades in school, did a great deal of baby-sitting for her mother, who was a single parent, and also held down a part-time job at a local drugstore. Some of Denise's earnings went to buy school clothes and pay for some weekend entertainment, but much of it went to her mother to help with the bills.

For a year Denise had been saving *everything* she earned to go on a French Club trip to Paris and other areas of France. The trip was a constant source of conversation with friends, and it filled her with daydreams and wonderful fantasies.

One month before the scheduled departure to France, Denise's mother informed her that their old furnace had to be replaced. Her mother needed most of Denise's recent savings to help pay the huge bill. Denise was heartbroken, but she understood her mother's problem and graciously gave her the money. Denise then notified the French Club advisor that she could not go on the trip.

One night, about a week later, Denise overheard her mother talking to her boyfriend on the phone. During the course of that phone conversation, her mother stated that it was no trouble loaning him the $500 he needed for a new motorcycle. He already had a very nice car. Denise was devastated. She came to me filled with a deep-burning sense of betrayal. The "Why me?" that justifiably came out of Denise's mouth was a hard one to answer.

Alice

Alice had spent a horrible school year being teased by a group of girls about her big nose. She could not handle one more day of her nickname—"Wicked

Witch of the West." Over the summer Alice begged her parents for plastic surgery—a "nose-job"—and by August her parents scraped together the money for the expensive surgery. The first day of school Alice raced to get there, being so proud of her new appearance. That first week, the same group of girls came up with a new nickname—"nose-job"—and proceeded to again tease Alice.

Alice took her life that same weekend. She was 13 years old. When will we learn that teasing can be murder in more than one sense of the word?

Secret givens

There are some givens that are especially tough and cause much trauma, primarily because they are family or personal secrets. These secret givens can seem even more unfair and are more destructive than others, and they can lead you to *scream* "Why me?" Let me share with you a list of the most common secret givens I have witnessed:

1. A chemically dependent parent or sibling.
2. Suspecting that you yourself are chemically dependent.
3. A physically abusive parent or sibling.
4. A sexually abusive parent or sibling.
5. Suspecting that you yourself are abusive.
6. A mentally ill parent or sibling.
7. Suspecting that you yourself are mentally ill.
8. A terminal illness within the family.
9. Homosexuality within the family.
10. Suspecting that you yourself are homosexual.

These and other secret givens are capable of demolishing your self-esteem, your hopes and dreams, your faith, and your whole family. These secret givens can turn your life, and the lives of your family members, into a real demolition derby.

When does "Why me?" become a killer?

I believe that "Why me?" has the potential of becoming a "killer question," a growing pain that can rip someone apart at the emotional seams, under the following conditions:

1. When you *believe* that it will never change.
2. When you *believe* that something cannot be forgiven or forgotten.
3. When you are so angry you feel like a volcano.
4. When you feel that you hate God.
5. When you feel you have no options or choices.
6. When you are exhausted physically.
7. When you are depressed emotionally.
8. When you are spiritually cynical.
9. When you panic.
10. When the pain is unbearable, and there appears to be nobody to talk to.

Under any of these conditions, "Why me?" can become too hot to handle.

God knows!

After this, Job opened his mouth and cursed the day of his birth. He said:

"May the day of my birth perish,
  and the night it was said, 'A boy is born!'

> That day—may it turn to darkness;
> may God above not care about it;
> may no light shine upon it."
>
> (Job 3:1-4)

> About the ninth hour Jesus cried out in a loud voice, *"Eloi, Eloi, lama sabachthani?"*—which means, "My God, my God, why have you forsaken me?"
>
> (Matt. 27:46)

The question "Why me?" is a part of life; it is part of being human, even for Jesus himself. At first it may not help to know you aren't alone, but I really believe that over time it is important to know you aren't crazy or weird or strange, *but just human.* Job wasn't nuts, he was just furious with life and as angry as he could be with God. Job felt it was his right to explode at God. He was simply human, and he just couldn't handle any more pain. "Why me?" is a question our hearts ask when the pain or hurt or fear is overflowing.

Initially it may not be very comforting to know that Christ has borne the pain of that question "Why me?" but think about it for awhile. Think about a Savior who *does* know your pain and who *does* fully understand being treated unfairly. Think about a Savior whose love for you is so full, so complete, that he will listen to you even when you need to rant and rave. Could you have a better friend? Could you ask for anyone to be more?

"So what? So he knows my pain—that doesn't change a thing about my situation!" As I said, at first you might say, "Who cares?" to knowing you are not alone, but I believe if you let Jesus' closeness, his love and his understanding, soak in for a bit, you will feel the difference. To know, to *really know* you are not alone and that Jesus does share your pain, is a miracle, a miracle of grace. Grace is the unconditional love of God, a love without any "I will only love you *if*. . . ." Grace is the reality of knowing Jesus Christ is always at your side. Even when you feel most alone, he is with you! Even when you feel most angry, he is with you! Even when you feel most beaten, he is with you!

Read these words from Isaiah 53 and consider how they express Jesus' love for you. Think about the "faith fact" that grace is the *ultimate given in life:*

> Surely he took up our infirmities
> and carried our sorrows,
> yet we considered him stricken by God,
> smitten by him, and afflicted.
> But he was pierced for our transgressions,
> he was crushed for our iniquities;
> the punishment that brought us peace was upon him,
> and by his wounds we are healed.
> We all, like sheep, have gone astray,
> each of us has turned to his own way;
> and the Lord has laid on him
> the iniquity of us all.
>
> (Isa. 53:4-6)

You are not alone! I am not alone! That is a miracle, and that miracle is an answer to the question "Why me?"

Through Jesus' eyes

> God saw all that he had made, and it was very good. And there was evening and there was morning—the sixth day.
>
> (Gen. 1:31)

One thing I will ask you to do quite often is to look at yourself or your situation through Jesus' eyes. I do this, not to have you play some kind of religious game, but because I believe it can help give you a more honest viewpoint. Just think what it is like right now to have Jesus at your side. How does he see you? hear you? How does he feel about your behavior? Take your time. Can you really feel Christ at your side? He's there. Can you see yourself through his eyes?

Through Jesus' eyes, how do your givens look? Do you find that Jesus, for the most part, likes what he sees? Could he care less about big feet, or the inability to do a cartwheel, or making a basket from the top of the key? Is Jesus dwelling on the best of who you are? Are you surprised to find him much more forgiving of your flaws than you are? Is Jesus reminding you that you are not the reason, or the excuse, for other people's abusive behavior? How do you feel about Jesus liking what he sees, loving you for who you are, and forgiving you for your mistakes? Don't you feel better about you now? Is that OK? If not, why not? Can you accept the love of God? Can you accept that in Jesus' eyes you are good and fine and beautiful and much more than just OK?

Tough love

> And our hope for you is firm, because we know that just as you share in our sufferings, so also you share in our comfort.
>
> (2 Cor. 1:7)

Jesus Christ does not curse your life with pain or hurt or bitter questions. However, if you believe in Jesus, you will accept these troubling times as opportunities to grow stronger in your faith. When you are able to tackle those difficult times by getting firmer in faith, you will realize what miracles Jesus can pull out of the pain:

1. You will grow in your understanding of Jesus' pain, and in doing so, grow closer to him.
2. You will grow in compassion for the pains and hurts of others.
3. You will become unafraid to face those "Why me?" times.
4. You will learn to patiently endure the hard times and know that Jesus will provide comfort for you in the end.
5. You will be unafraid of life and love, both of which require a lot of pain, hurt, and hardship.
6. You will have become more the disciple you were created to be: "If anyone would come after me, he must deny himself and take up his cross and follow me" (Matt. 16:24).

Even when you live in a home that is abusive chemically, physically, or sexually—a situation that Jesus hates just as much as you do—this too can become a time of great personal and faith growth. But please, don't take this to mean you should not seek help. Part of that growth is realizing that you need the help of others to escape a horrible situation.

You will make it!

When you ask the question, "Why me?" often you may feel as if there is no answer, no solution, no love to ease the pain, and no hope for a better tomorrow. When you feel so fragile and vulnerable, it is hard to even imagine having the energy to go on, and sometimes, for some of you, even one more day seems out of the question. At such frightening times, you must remember that the Holy Spirit is working daily to restore your happiness and your hope. There are those who can help you. Seek them out. When you feel as barren as a tree in midwinter, remember that the Spirit is working below the surface to create the blossoms of a new spring. You will make it! Hang on! The beautiful buds of new life are being quietly fed by the Spirit, and even if you cannot see the Spirit's expert gardening, please do trust that it is taking place.

> Then Jesus told him, "Because you have seen me, you have believed; blessed are those who have not seen and yet have believed."
>
> (John 20:29)

2

"WILL ANYTHING EVER BE THE SAME AGAIN?"

The question "Will anything ever be the same again?" usually is asked when a person has experienced a *dramatic departure or ending or a significant loss.* The loss of someone close—by death or divorce or by simply moving away—feels like someone pouring cold water over the opening from which a tooth has been removed. My wife once described how she was unable to celebrate Christmas for several years following the death of her mother: "I would hide in the bathroom of wherever the family get-together was being held and sob into a towel. The rest of the day I would try to compensate by being too happy, too loud, too funny. I felt that without Mom, the main reason we had for feeling like family was gone. I seemed to have buried Christmas right with her." The pain of losses and endings can be shattering and can leave you feeling as though your life's "jigsaw puzzle" was just thrown up in the air. It is an overwhelming feeling, like having the wind knocked out of you, and it is an experience filled with a fear—"Will anything ever be the same again?"

Divorces

Over the years I have learned that the bottom line when it comes to divorce is that you would do almost anything to keep it from happening. Divorce—even when it ends a lousy marriage—still creates great hardship for the young person whose parents are splitting. No matter how many times I have heard some youths say, "It really doesn't bother me that much," I have also noticed the frequency of wet eyes or look-away stares that accompany the comment. Divorce is a real test, and for those of you who feel like you are flunking, it can become a life-threatening event. Let me share with you some of the experiences of a few teens I counseled while the parents were going through a divorce. As you read their views, try to relate to the depth of the pain they felt and the huge changes the divorce had forced on their lives.

MATT: "What can I do? My family just died." Matt was 15 when his parents split, and for Matt the key issue was the loss of his family as he had always known it. "It feels so strange to think of never eating dinner together as a family or celebrating a birthday or Thanksgiving or just going on a family vacation." Divorce in a very real way is the death of a family, and that leaves a hole inside as deep as a canyon.

DAWN: "I wonder if Dad will stop loving me next." Dawn struggled with the reality that her father, who always claimed to be in love with Dawn's mother, was now not only out of love with his wife, but in love with someone else. No matter how her father tried to tell Dawn that his love for her would never end, for Dawn her father's guarantees just did not hold much weight anymore. Would she ever trust his love again?

BOB: "I had to grow up too fast. I got cheated out of being just a normal kid." For Bob, whose parents divorced when he was eight, the divorce had stolen his childhood. He had to become the man of the house long before he either wanted that role or felt ready to handle it. Bob grew up quickly as a result of the divorce, and he was often affirmed for his maturity at such a young age. However, on the inside, Bob resented that forced maturity and often grieved over not getting to grow up more slowly.

ELLEN: "I'll die if I have to choose between them." Ellen, like so many children of divorce, felt as if she was being pulled apart by her parents' competing for her affections. There is nothing worse in a divorce than when children are used as pawns in their parents' emotional chess match. To be so used, as Ellen was, is a wicked punishment to receive for a situation that is not their fault.

FRANK: "If only I had been a better son." Frank was convinced that his brief involvement with drugs and a few semesters of poor grades were the reasons for his parents' divorce. His feelings of guilt and grief were overwhelming. Even though I tried to reassure him that their marriage had problems far more severe than dealing with his brief rebellion, Frank remained convinced that it was all his fault. Frank attempted suicide twice during the first year following his parents' divorce. He is now reconciled to the fact, after a lot of counseling and praying, that his parents' marriage had gone bad long before he did.

Divorce certainly leads many young people to ask, "Will anything ever be the same again?" and forces some of you to face a pain you may not be ready to handle. Yes, most kids adjust to a divorce, but the emotional and spiritual price is much higher than we have been led to believe. We all need to take more seriously the impact of divorce, no matter how common it is these days. Though I am not personally opposed to all divorces, as some marriages cannot be saved, I do consider divorce to be a devastating blow to many young lives, and never an experience to be assumed as natural or normal.

Death

Two weeks before my wedding, I found myself in the unusual position of asking my soon-to-be-wife, "Don't you think it's time to buy a wedding dress?" My wife turned away, avoided the question, and changed the subject. I continued to question her until finally Christine burst forth, "Picking out a wedding dress is something you are supposed to do with your mother!" Twenty years had passed since Chris's mother had died, but there were times when the loss was still as painful and present as if it had happened yesterday.

For a young person such a loss can be a brutal blow. Death can feel like a knockout punch, leaving you without the will to get up or even the breath to get going. Over the last 10 years of ministry, I have had to share such losses with many young people, and I have found their reactions are fairly consistent. The reactions, by the way, vary according to the type of death (by disease or drunk driving, for example), the age of the person lost, and the kind of relationship—parent, sibling, extended family, friend, or acquaintance. Let me share with you some fairly common reactions to death, but remember you may have felt, or feel differently, as this is definitely an incomplete list.

1. *I feel responsible somehow.*
   From time to time, you may have wished that your parents or brothers or sisters were dead. You may have even told them flat out that you wished they were gone. It is normal for you to fantasize their absence, or even to get so angry that you say things you don't mean, like, "I wish you were dead." In talking to adolescents who felt this way, I have had to remind them that they just aren't that powerful, and that death isn't caused by a "curse." Your words, your rebellious

behavior, even your silent wishes, are not the cause of someone's death.

2. *Parents are supposed to always be there.*
Some of you who have experienced the death of a parent are overwhelmed by the loss of what you had always believed to be one of life's basic assumptions—that Mom and Dad would always be there. We often think of parents as a guaranteed given in life, and it is a tragic mistake to do so. For those of you who have lost a parent, there is a feeling of being ready to burst with the cry, "Unfair!"

3. *But they were so young.*
When death hits someone young—a baby, a child, a peer—it is even harder to accept. Most adolescents assume that death is reserved for elderly people, and when it hits someone quite young, it forces them to face the fact that death is not selective. Recently, in a community where I was working, there were four teenagers killed in traffic accidents over one weekend. They were all from the same high school. Their classmates were stunned by the loss and the awareness of just how fragile life is *at all ages*.

4. *They didn't deserve this!*
Good people die, and this is one of the harshest facts of life. It is even harder to accept the fact that good people at times die terrible, even brutal, deaths. Like those people who observed

Jesus on the cross, you, too, will at times be shocked by the injustice of death.

5. *I never even thought about death.*
Every day you are living, you are also dying. This is a fact of life. Sometimes, the only way we become aware of that fact is through the death of someone we love or care about. It forces us all to face the reality that death is part of life.

Other losses

Besides divorce and death, there are also other losses that can be equally difficult. The loss of a pet may seem like nothing to many people, but for some of you, it is like you lost part of yourself. Having to move, especially while in high school, means ripping up roots, leaving you nothing to hold on to. Doing something really stupid, like driving drunk or cheating on a major exam or getting caught in a whopper of a lie, can cause you to lose self-respect, and that too is a horrible loss. To find out that an adult you have always respected is having an affair or is chemically dependent or abusive can also be terribly upsetting. To be so angry with God, for whatever the reason, that you feel you have lost faith, can also result in the loss of hope, and that is a major defeat.

One of the toughest losses for a teen to overcome is when a romantic relationship that you dreamed would last forever somehow suddenly ends. When you fall in love you pour your whole being into that relationship, and the other person becomes your world. Love is so powerful, the fall so deep and so long, that you are convinced you cannot live without the one you love. We are still a bit like Romeo and Juliet, and though I am in my mid-30s, I still know the fall of love can be terrifying, and the crash that often comes at the bottom hurts like no other pain I've ever known. It is a mistake to make another person your god, yet falling in love can make it almost impossible not to. But whenever you make another person your god, the relationship is doomed. The difference between worship and love is a big one, but one that the heart at romantic times has a tough time discerning. Don't suffocate your relationship with excessive love. Be wise in your loving and in your "falling."

A killing question

"Will anything ever be the same again?" can be deadly for a young person under the following conditions:

1. When you somehow, no matter how irrational the reason, feel *responsible* for the loss.
2. When you have experienced multiple endings over a rather brief period of time.
3. When the loss is uniquely tragic, the death violent, or the ending extremely *senseless* by everyone's standards.
4. When you experience the loss of a *first love,* which is so overwhelming that it feels like you've lost *all* love—the love of the whole world and the love you have for yourself.
5. When the loss has been *denied* totally *for an extensive period of time.*
6. When your relationship to God has become so

coated with a feeling of betrayal that you believe you can no longer pray.

7. When those you love and trust the most refuse to listen or to take your feelings seriously, or worse yet, tell you just to be strong.

Grief must be admitted, claimed, experienced, endured, and conquered, but that can only come when you are willing to let Jesus Christ share that grief with you. Again, Jesus will not make the grief evaporate overnight, but he can give you the courage to plow through those low points in your life.

Jesus' tears

Everyone marveled at Kirk's handling of his mother's death by cancer. In fact, everyone commented to me about how strong he was at the funeral, never shedding a tear. I saw Kirk's so-called strength as a warning for disaster.

At his high school graduation, Kirk was overcome with sadness, realizing that his mother, more than anyone, would have made the night special, for she alone took such pride in his academic accomplishments. Later that week, after attending a friend's sister's funeral and having a few beers, Kirk came home and slashed his wrists.

One of the biggest mistakes made in handling losses is by trying to be strong, which usually means denying our feelings, avoiding our pain, or ignoring the messages of our hearts. Take a moment to consider Jesus' griefs—yes, he too grieves—and see what you might learn:

> And after she had said this, she went back and called her sister Mary aside. "The Teacher is here," she said,

> "and is asking for you." When Mary heard this, she got up quickly and went to him. Now Jesus had not yet entered the village, but was still at the place where Martha had met him. When the Jews who had been with Mary in the house, comforting her, noticed how quickly she got up and went out, they followed her, supposing she was going to the tomb to mourn there.
>
> When Mary reached the place where Jesus was and saw him, she fell at his feet and said, "Lord, if you had been here, my brother would not have died."
>
> When Jesus saw her weeping, and the Jews who had come along with her also weeping, he was deeply moved in spirit and troubled. "Where have you laid him?" he asked.
>
> "Come and see, Lord," they replied.
>
> Jesus wept.
>
> Then the Jews said, "See how he loved him!"
>
> (John 11:28-36)

Though the story is unfortunately brief, we still get a clear picture of a Christ who grieves, a Christ whose tears flow easily, a Christ who claims the great pain of his loss.

Jesus' tears have become for me a symbol of grief. His tears tell me that grief is normal and that true strength is found in true feeling. Jesus' tears tell me that faith includes pain, but my pain is understood, my grief is embraced, my agony received by a God of endless compassion. Jesus' tears tell me once again, *"You are not alone."*

Grieving tips

The following tips on grief come out of my own experience and what I believe the example of Jesus' grief offers us. Everyone grieves in their own way, but the kinds of feelings are common. It is good to remember these things:

1. Remember, grief is normal.
2. There is no time line on grief.
3. Tears offer a sense of cleansing renewal.
4. Jesus can handle your anger.
5. *You* are not the cause.
6. You need to talk about your loss with someone you trust, as well as with Jesus.
7. Your memories are eternal.
8. Life is eternal.
9. You are forgiven for those times you wish you would have said and done things differently.
10. Healing takes time.
11. Jesus knows that change hurts.
12. You will find the strength to accept the changes that life imposes on you, if you only believe in Jesus.
13. Pray without ceasing.
14. The resurrection is real.
15. Jesus wants so badly to be there for you. Please come to him as often as you like.

I believe that Jesus Christ will help you use your grief as a time of learning and as a means of maturing. When you face the pain of a loss or an ending, you also face what really matters to you, what you value deeply. Grief seldom comes over losses that are trivial or endings that just don't matter much. Because grief is reserved for losses and endings that are significant, it also becomes a teacher of priorities, values, and standards. No matter how hard it is to honestly face the pain of grief, that pain will produce an awareness of what you believe is of great worth in life. To know what you value, to know what you believe in and what you need and want from life, is a valuable lesson often only taught by grief.

Something stays the same

> Jesus Christ is the same yesterday and today and forever.
>
> (Heb. 13:8)

Even in the midst of great change or during times when huge holes are punctured in your world, there is one constant. Even when your whole spirit is crying "Will anything ever be the same again?" Jesus is there. Jesus Christ is a constant source of comfort, care, concern, hope, healing, and health. Especially when you are struggling with a death, it is critical that you remember that Jesus was with you before you were born, and is with you every step of your life, and will be with you forever. And those you have loved and lost are also in the hands of a loving God.

3
"WILL I EVER BE SOMEBODY REALLY *SPECIAL?*"

A friend once told me of a blue ribbon he had won as a five-year-old at the summer playground pet show. His pet hamster was awarded "best squeak" in the show. How thrilled my friend had been with his Coke bottle cap hammered flat and spray painted a bright gold, with a long flowing blue ribbon attached by a glob of glue! Racing home, he proudly displayed his medal to his mother.

"Who else won?" she asked.

"Well," he replied, "Jimmy won for biggest dog, and Eddie won for his cat's tail, and Ernie won for best chameleon, and. . . ." Suddenly it dawned on him that every friend he had, in fact every person at the pet show, had won a blue ribbon. "Even Sally won for most silent animal, and she brought a dumb stuffed rabbit!" Throwing the ribbon to the floor, my friend exclaimed, "This stupid thing isn't special—we all got one!"

His mother, retrieving it from the floor, said quietly, "No, the ribbon *is* special, but your playground leaders thought you were *all* special." Still, for my friend, the gold bottle cap was tarnished, and the ribbon was a frayed and faded blue.

We all want to feel that we stand out or that something about us makes us truly unique, really special. I can't tell you how many times as an adolescent I dreamed of scoring the winning basket from half court with one second left on the clock or driving up to the Prom in a black Corvette, or giving the valedictory graduation speech, or being discovered by the Green Bay Packers or a Hollywood talent scout, or starring in a Broadway musical, or being the beloved doctor serving the masses in Africa. I wanted to do something spectacular, I wanted to be extraordinary, and I wanted my blue ribbon to be for best in the show, period.

I think such fantasies are normal. However, recently I have discovered that for many of you such fantasies are really expectations, and that for some of you the thought of being ordinary is disgusting and the desire to be extraordinary, all consuming. I have conducted countless workshops this past year, dealing with the general theme of "adolescent pressures." As part of these workshops, I ask the kids involved how they would feel if they were told that they were *common—ordinary—average* and that their future would be likewise. Let me share with you some of the reactions I received, and then let me offer you my conclusions.

Most of the kids I dealt with in these workshops were what I call high achievers. The majority of these kids were highly motivated to succeed, and they took their lives, their grades, and their futures very seriously. Their responses give dramatic testimony to the repulsion for the ordinary in many young minds. Remember, the question was, "How would you feel if you were told you were pretty common, fairly average, just ordinary, and that your future would be about the same?" Here's what they had to say:

"like a complete loser"
"a total waste"
"worthless"
"sort of hopeless"
"ultimate boredom"
"like the floor—go ahead, walk on me!"
"why bother"
"a slave"
"unbelievably disappointed"
"a carcass"
"expendable."

It seems to me that for a considerable number of you, especially if you are what our culture calls an "achiever type," to be thought of as ordinary, common, or average is enough to make you wonder whether it's worth getting up in the morning.

Consider this conversation I had recently with a 16-year-old I will call Kevin:

BILL: Aren't you excited about your future?
KEVIN: Sort of.
BILL: Just sort of?
KEVIN: Well, it won't be anything too great.

BILL: How do you know?

KEVIN: I just do. I'm just average. I get OK grades and stuff. I'm OK in some sports. But I just don't do anything great.

BILL: I think you'll have a good future. You're a really good person.

KEVIN: Yeah, but big deal. What difference will that make?

BILL: I think it's a big deal.

KEVIN: I know *you* do, but nobody else does. I'll probably just have a pretty normal, boring life.

BILL: What does that mean?

KEVIN: I'll get a job. I'll get married. I'll have some kids. I'll play on some silly softball team with my old high school friends, you know. . . .

BILL: Well, what would you like your future to look like?

KEVIN: I guess I'm just like everyone else. I'd like to make a lot of money. Travel a lot. Marry the perfect girl. Have a Porsche. You know—the good life.

BILL: So it doesn't matter to you at all that you're a good person, a good friend, and that you'll probably be a good husband and a good father? It doesn't matter that you are, at least in my way of thinking, a good Christian?

KEVIN: I'd like to say it does matter, but down deep, Pastor Bill, it really doesn't. I've just always dreamed of being popular, a "winner."

BILL: You *are* a winner.

KEVIN: You know what I mean—wear the right clothes, go to the right school, drive the right car, know the right people, live in the right neighborhood.

BILL: I know many people who have all of that who aren't one bit happy, Kevin, and to be honest, some of them are not very good people.

KEVIN: Yeah, but I'd still like to. . . .

BILL: Even if you were unhappy on the inside?

KEVIN: The truth?

BILL: The truth.

KEVIN: Yeah, even if I wasn't happy on the inside, which I doubt.

No matter how much I wanted to talk Kevin out of his idea of the good life, I knew in my heart that not only was he telling me the truth, but that his perception of the good life is a "truth" for many young people today. But a future that places no value in being a good friend, a good mate or parent, a good neighbor, or a good citizen, is a future that is doomed to being terribly unhappy. If the good life today means giving up on goodness, then I hope Kevin, and all of you, will be wise enough not to swallow such a huge *lie.* It is my faith in Jesus Christ that makes me know that Kevin's idea of a "winner" is false. It's a lie. The truth is that just being an ordinary disciple can be life's most extraordinary accomplishment.

Judy

Brothers, think of what you were when you were called. Not many of you were wise by human standards; not many were influential; not many were of

> noble birth. But God chose the foolish of the world to shame the wise; God chose the weak things of the world to shame the strong. He chose the lowly things of this world and the despised things—and the things that are not—to nullify the things that are, so that no one may boast before him. It is because of him that you are in Christ Jesus, who has become for us wisdom from God—that is, our righteousness, holiness and redemption. Therefore, as it is written: "Let him who boasts boast in the Lord."
>
> (1 Cor. 1:26-31)

The church was never this full, not even on Easter or Christmas Eve. Three things from that service stand out in my mind. First, the singing literally raised the roof. On the last hymn, "Joy to the World," a rather unusual selection for the month of June and a funeral, the congregation sang as if fueled by some inner fire. Secondly, there was a mood of closeness, as if this huge throng of people was one family. And finally, when leaving the church, I was stopped by a little boy from the neighborhood who had noticed the hearse and the "mob." He asked if someone famous had died. I laughed and said yes. He got wide eyed. "Who?" he asked. I knew he wouldn't understand, but I replied, "This person was a different kind of famous."

Judy was a different kind of famous, but to those of us who loved her, she will be remembered far longer than some movie star or celebrity. What was Judy's claim to fame? Why did her funeral attract so many friends? Judy was a wonderful wife and mother, and her family reflected her powerful ability to love. Judy was always Judy—never phoney, always honest and fair. Judy was an exceptionally loyal friend, especially when any of us was at a really low point. Judy constantly sacrified her time, her energies, and her money for what she believed in. She had strong convictions. She hated bigotry, stood up for the poor, and was violently opposed to the use of drugs. Judy was committed. She was deeply involved in her church, her choir, her neighborhood, and she was always active in some service project. She drove for "Meals on Wheels." She served at a local soup kitchen on Friday nights. She visited members of our congregation who were ill or homebound, often delivering flowers on Sundays. She never forgot a birthday or an anniversary. She always knew what you were feeling without your having to tell her. Judy could make you laugh, and she would cry with you.

Judy was a different kind of famous, but of all the wonderful qualities that made her *extraordinary,* the one that stands out for me was her quiet faith. She never was one to ram her faith down your throat or make you feel that her faith was vastly superior. She simply always let you know how blessed she felt herself to be, and how thankful she was to Jesus Christ for just about everything.

Judy was an extraordinarily ordinary woman. By the world's standards she wasn't much at all. She had no great power or wealth or notoriety. She hadn't accomplished anything that would be recorded in a history book or even noted by a newspaper. Still, Judy made such an impact on so many lives, and her love transformed so many hearts on so many occasions. I wish Kevin could have been at her funeral. Then he would know what a real "winner" is all about, and what makes for a life that really is "the good life."

Real riches

> "Do not store up for yourselves treasures on earth, where moth and rust destroy, and where thieves break in to steal. But store up for yourselves treasures in heaven, where moth and rust do not destroy, and where thieves do not break in and steal. For where your treasure is, there your heart will be also. . . . No one can serve two masters. Either he will hate the one and love the other, or he will be devoted to the one and despise the other. You cannot serve both God and money."
>
> (Matt. 6:19-21, 24)

Jesus Christ came into this world and revealed to us a revolutionary understanding of riches. He forced us to face the truth that we will never be measured by the width of our pocketbook or the length of our car, but always and only by our relationship to God. Jesus scorched us with an insight, a blazing truth, that God measures us by yardsticks of faith, love, and discipleship, and never for the size of our bank account.

Jesus came into this world in a lowly fashion, in a most ordinary setting, surrounded by mostly ordinary folks. So it would continue to be for most of his life, and almost all of his ministry. Jesus was the champion of ordinary, for he enabled those who had nothing by the world's standards to know they could still be rich in the eyes of God. Let me try to summarize for you what I think it means to be rich in the eyes of God, or how we might learn to store up some riches in heaven:

1. You are rich whenever you forgive someone.
2. You are rich whenever you share what you have, especially that which actually hurts to share.
3. You are rich whenever you make a sacrifice of time, talent, tithes, especially a sacrifice that hurts.
4. You are rich whenever you choose to pray.
5. You are rich whenever you choose to worship.
6. You are rich whenever you work at your loving.
7. You are rich whenever you try to make peace within a relationship, at home or school, or in your neighborhood or world.
8. You are rich whenever you strive to ease the suffering—emotional or physical—of another human being.
9. You are rich whenever you strive to bring justice and equality to our society.
10. You are rich whenever you put the needs of others before your own.
11. You are rich whenever you put Jesus first in your life.

To be rich in the eyes of Jesus is to be genuinely extraordinary and to know at last that being really *special* means nothing more, or less, than being a *disciple.*

4 "HOW MANY HAPPY ADULTS DO YOU KNOW?"

Matt and Shannon were acting out a dramatic role play before the entire youth group. They had the difficult task of trying to explain why they each had gotten involved in an affair, both playing the parts of married adults. Shannon declared in her defense, "My life was just so boring, so predictable, such a stupid rut. Everything, day after day, was the same. The affair just spiced things up." Matt, in a sarcastic tone, echoed Shannon, "My marriage is boring, my job is boring, being an adult is *boring, boring, boring!*"

After the role play was over, I asked for comments from the group. I especially wanted them to tell me if I was correct in thinking that they felt adulthood, especially marriage, was a pretty dull experience. Reluctantly at first, but then with some real intensity, the group told me that they did think of growing up in pretty boring terms, they truly believed adulthood was a rather bland event.

A family came to me for counseling. The mother described their situation as a "complete breakdown in communication with our daughter." The daughter Nancy was going through a tough time. She had just broken up with her boyfriend and was being cruelly ignored by her former group of girlfriends. Those girlfriends had not liked the boy Nancy was dating, and even though she was no longer dating him, they made it a point to leave her out of every plan and conversation. It is fair to say that Nancy's unhappiness was spilling over at home, and that often her parents were scapegoats.

However, what really captured my attention was an outburst from Nancy during one session. Her father had simply stated that he and Nancy's mother "just wanted her to be happy, that was all." Nancy's explosion caught everyone by surprise.

"You always say that," she said. "You always say you want me to be happy. Well, I'm sorry, I'm not happy. Is that a sin? Anyway, are you two all that happy? You never talk to each other, except about money. Half the time you are yelling. Mom, you sit home every day and watch soap operas and drink wine all afternoon. You always tell me about what you could have been. And Dad, what about you? You hate your job. You only seem happy when you are alone listening to your police radio. Neither of you have any good friends, at least not that I can tell, not friends you can just drop in on and really talk with. We eat dinner together, and all you two do is complain and complain and complain. First it's about taxes or people on welfare or the phone bill, or it's about my grades, or Donny's (her brother). Is that what you want, for me to be happy like you two?"

Nancy's parents were honestly stunned by their daughter's words, but they were mature enough to admit that she was for the most part right. They had never stopped to consider how negative they sounded or how unhappy they probably appeared to be. However, through several more sessions they were able to share with Nancy a great many activities and experiences that gave them great pleasure and deep satisfaction. Nancy was thrilled to know her parents better, and she began to realize that though they were not perfectly happy, her folks were quite content. Even more importantly, Nancy's mother vowed to do something more constructive on her afternoons, and her father agreed to spend less time glued to a police radio.

Over the past few years, I have become more and more aware of how many of you think as Nancy did—that adults are basically unhappy. "How many happy adults do you know?" is a question I have found many of you to be asking, and it points to your belief that adulthood is not something to look forward to. I have also come to the realization that we adults, myself included, have done a terrible job of telling you what gives meaning to our lives. We just haven't shared with you our moments of joy and goosebumps or times of stomach-twirling excitement. We haven't told you what makes our hearts leap with anticipation. We have talked too much about how to make it financially in life and not nearly enough about how to make it emotionally and spiritually. I sincerely believe that you want to know less about the good life and more about how to make life really good.

In a way I think it is healthy that so many of you have faced a truth about adulthood, and that is that adults are human. We are often frightened, foolish, childish, vulnerable, wrong, faithless, hypocritical, conceited, arrogant, boring, bored, stagnant, and the worst of sinners. Still, being humans, we are also capable of being compassionate, forgiving, self-sacrificing, faithful, committed, wise, warm, wonderful, risk-takers, star-followers, honest, authentic, mature, passionate, and even Christlike. Being *just* a human being isn't so bad, for human beings are capable of wonderful things. Even though a major task of maturing is to face your limitations, your pains and heartaches, your conflicts and crises, your ruts and boring routines, we humans are still capable of creating lives of dignity, lives of simple splendors, and lives infested with love. Being human, my friends, is not a curse of boredom. It is a blessing of a rich and vibrant opportunity to choose to live and to love to the fullest. Even though I am pleased so many of you know the truth that adults are fragile and, at times, quite unhappy human beings, I think that you need also to claim the truth that adults can be creatures of unbelivable courage and joy. We adults can definitely be both, and at the same time too.

Now, it's time for me to tell you about what makes *me* happy and probably many other adults as well. On behalf of these adults and myself, I apologize for not having shared my happiness earlier, because, you see, there is much that does make us happy. Here is my very incomplete list:

- The feeling I get when I creep into my son's room late at night, and just stare in wonder.
- The times when I have felt so distant from my wife, yet when I look at her, I melt and fall in love again, simply because I cherish so deeply the history we have shared and are creating, and because I am certain I could never enjoy life as much without her.
- Walking through a forest of fall leaves right after a rain shower.
- When the snow comes down in Goliath flakes, and I try to catch them on my tongue.
- Hot coffee and a newspaper.
- A cold shower in August and a scalding tub in February.
- Candlelight.
- Times of laughter, like when the woman sitting next to me on an airplane responded to the captain's announcement that we were at 33,000 feet with the words, "So who's measuring?"
- Watching people at airports or bus stations or at a ball game.
- A good movie and a bucket of popcorn dripping with butter.
- The cleansing of a good long cry, or a good long prayer.
- Swimming and sledding.
- The sound of a French horn.
- Racing down a hill on a bike.
- The smell of homemade bread.

- A big fire in a fireplace and a ton of memories.
- Afghans and hugs.
- A good political debate or a serious discussion on ethics.
- Watching children playing in puddles.
- People who are passionate about their dreams, their views, their faith.
- Playing "Scrabble" or "Password."
- Walking in a windstorm.
- Blizzards.
- Early morning talks with my mom and late night talks with my dad.
- My collection of sweaters.

I take great joy in writing this list because I could just keep on going. I haven't even mentioned my work, my writing, my friends. At times I really need to count my blessings, to just sit down and realize how good God has been to me *overall.* At times you need to do the same, or at least know that in time your list, too, will grow. My list, like so many adult lists, might sound too simple, too sentimental, but believe me it is a list of wishes that have come true, of life experienced at its most satisfying.

These days, it can seem pretty hard to locate a role model or find a genuine hero, but it isn't impossible. I ask you to keep looking. If your looking is long and penetrating, I sincerely believe you will find many folks who are worthy of hero or model status. They may not be societal superstars but they just may be people whose simple lives stand for mercy and justice and peace, people whose lives are testimonies to the truth of Jesus Christ. Deep in the eyes is a pool of tears, tears of sorrow and of joy, and there one will find the reflection of goodness that is so worthy of following. Look long! Look deep!

Bowl removal

> "You are the light of the world. A city on a hill cannot be hidden. Neither do people light a lamp and put it under a bowl. Instead they put it on its stand, and it gives light to everyone in the house. In the same way, let your light shine before men, that they may see your good deeds and praise your Father in heaven."
>
> (Matt. 5:14-16)

I have just confessed that we adults have done a terrible job in making you aware of what brings us joy, what makes us happy or hopeful, and I guess it could be said that we adults often choose to live under "bowls." We seldom put ourselves on the "lampstand," so you never get to see the "light" that many of us radiate. I'd like to suggest that you might be of tremendous assistance in removing the bowls that cover so many adult lives, including those of your parents and grandparents, aunts and uncles, teachers, ministers, priests, coaches, counselors, or neighbors.

Do you realize that you might just remove that bowl with a single solitary question? If you are willing to ask a question, or even two, and then genuinely listen, I think you will have managed to put an unsuspecting adult (adults seldom suspect you are interested enough to ask) on a lampstand, where, I might add, so many adults belong. Here are some sample questions:

1. What were your parents like?
2. Could you try to explain your faith to me?

3. How does it feel to fall in love?
4. What do you look for in a friend?
5. How would you define success?
6. Have you ever experienced a miracle?
7. When do you pray?
8. What hurts you the most to hear someone say about you?
9. Are you ever lonely?
10. How do you handle your anger?
11. What is your biggest fear?
12. What is your most significant accomplishment to date?
13. What has been your biggest disappointment?
14. Is Jesus Christ real for you?
15. How do you cope with failure?
16. Do you have any secret dreams or goals?
17. Have you ever wanted to end it all?
18. Are you ever depressed?
19. How do you think other people see you?
20. How do you think God sees you?

I not only believe that you can help get adults out from under their bowls, but if you are interested and loving enough to put them on a lampstand, you will discover that there are many happy adults out there, many adults worth admiring. Out from under our bowls, you might find many of us downright enjoyable, and you might even begin to think of adulthood with excitement again.

Wisdom

Is not wisdom found among the aged?
Does not long life bring understanding?

To God belong wisdom and power;
counsel and understanding are his.
(Job 12:12-13)

John always spoke of his father in a way that let you know he was his hero and that he felt immense pride for the man. During one youth group discussion I asked John what made his father so special to him, not knowing the intimacy I was asking John to share with the whole group. John paused for quite a long time, to me it seemed like a month, and finally spoke. "Well, my father is an alcoholic, and I am very proud of him for quitting. He never misses an AA meeting, and he always encourages us to go to Al-Anon. I just feel so glad that he was wise enough to not destroy his life and our family. He really has his act together. He couldn't be happier, and neither could I."

After John spoke, the whole group applauded, and John was moved to tears. It was a very special, and very happy moment for us all. John's father was wise, and maybe the real issue of adulthood isn't happiness, but wisdom. If you are wise, you are guaranteed to have many happy days.

Wisdom comes with age. That does not mean wisdom comes only to the old, or that you are never wise. Wisdom simply comes with the process of maturing, for maturation is that force in life that always reminds us we are not God and we are powerless without God. I have known 40-year-old individuals who display the maturity of 10-year-olds, and teens who exhibit the maturity of someone in their 60s. Wisdom grows in the "garden of maturation," a garden whose soil is made up of the understanding that it is the will of

God for humans to be human. If we are planted in that soil, we won't waste our lives trying to be anything but human, and we will be able to have a faith that knows the freedom that comes to those who claim their dependence on grace, the unconditional love of God. The roots of wisdom grow firm and deep, whereas the roots of success in our world couldn't be more shallow.

I want you to know something else about wisdom, something that may help you understand adults and make adults more worthy of admiration and imitation in your mind. The person who is wise often wears a particular kind of face, and that "look" of wisdom may fool you. You tend to measure happiness on the Richter scale of laughter, good times, parties, or pure excitement, and wisdom, on that scale, just doesn't measure up. Wisdom can be exciting, ecstatic even, but it tends to produce silence, solitude, a sensation of quiet and calm deep inside. Wisdom just isn't a "party animal." It is sort of a stay-at-home-and-read-a-good-book type of experience. Wisdom creates a peace in one's soul, a peace that passes all understanding, a sensation of being good friends with God, a feeling of being literally embraced by grace. Wisdom may not look like happiness, but the silent laughter of the soul, the quiet conversations with God, and the calm of knowing we are God's own children brings on a satisfaction so warm, well, it could melt a star.

Why am I telling you all this about wisdom? I guess it is because I think you might at times not notice the wisdom of adults, or you might mistake moments of peace as times of boredom. Worse yet, times when adult faith is bloated with adoration might look to you like an escape, or arrogance, or a giving up. Wisdom is a giving up, but it is a giving up of the mentality that wastes time building monuments to self and human power and spends no time building the kingdom of God on this earth. So, I simply ask that you notice wisdom. Look for it on the faces of adults and realize that some of those boring people marooned in the quicksand of adulthood just might be experiencing deep joy and satisfaction in knowing they are participating in the kingdom, in knowing they are right with God. Remember, if you are looking for heroes or role models, you need look no further than the face of wisdom.

5 "IS LIFE JUST AN ENDURANCE TEST THAT NOBODY EVER PASSES?"

At a dinner-dialog about a year and a half ago—a dinner-dialog being the inhaling of five or six pizzas by about 20 always-ravenous youths, followed by discussion on a chosen topic—several young people asked me why I had left Milwaukee to come to Long Island. I hesitated for a bit, but I decided that if I expected my youth groups to be honest with me, I had to be straight with them. So I responded slowly, "To be blunt, I was totally burned out." This statement brought on an avalanche of questions: "How do you get burned out? What *is* burnout? How do you get over it? Has Long Island helped? Are you burned out now? Could we tell if you were?"

I proceeded to do my best to explain to the group how I understood burnout. I listed the following feelings and experiences, as well as attitudes, as being signs of burnout:

1. You feel physically tired all of the time, even after sleep.
2. You feel hollow, without any energy or spark.
3. You begin to think of life as an *endless* series of duties, chores, and responsibilities.
4. You often feel used, even abused, by others, but primarily, you just feel taken for granted.
5. You never play, or take *re-creation* time.
6. You think life offers no rewards, that all the hard work just yields more work.
7. You feel every day is an exact clone of the day before.
8. You begin to believe things will never change, that past mistakes will continue to haunt you and that the future holds only the promise of more of the same.
9. You are furious over what you think is unfair or unjust treatment—by your job, your friends, your family, and your God.
10. You feel guilty for being so angry and for not having the strength to tough it out.

After I completed my rather lengthy description of burnout, I immediately noticed that heads were nodding, and faces were smeared with knowing looks. "That describes half the group here tonight," they said. And individuals responded, "Hearing that makes me feel old already." "Can someone 17 be burned out?" Some of the looks I got could have felled a buffalo at 200 yards. Sure, Grimbol, we adolescents don't really fall in love, we don't really experience stress or depression, and we have no reasons that would ever merit considering suicide. We are just fun loving, shallow, trite, space cadet kids, right? Their eyes told me loud and clear what they thought, and even more loudly how wrong I was. Yes, a 17-year-old can be burned out. Indeed, many of you are. I stood, and stand, corrected.

This particular youth group was probably an ideal one for youth burnout. These kids lived in a very affluent community of highly educated people. Their folks were ambitious achievers who expected their kids to follow in their productive and "use-your-potential" footsteps. Don't get me wrong. This was a place like thousands of other such suburban communities, a place where good, prosperous, hard-working, dedicated people try to create an environment that will help their children to flourish. The high school that most of these kids attended was a top-flight school, cranking out high SAT scores from its students and sending a vast majority of them off to college, a good chunk to the "best schools in the country." This was, however, the kind of setting where burnout so often occurs, both in adults and in adolescents. Even in my youth group there were faces of burnout, especially among the seniors. Out of 20 kids, three claimed some level of burnout. That's a pretty high percentage.

Since that dinner-dialog I have not only recognized burnout in a great many more adolescent faces, but I've realized how many adolescents I counseled over the past 10 years were also burnout victims. We need to acknowledge the very real presence of adolescent burnout, and we need to seriously consider the very real connection between burnout and contemplating suicide. For someone who feels hollow and exhausted, suicide can be very tempting and not at all frightening.

Let me share with you those factors I have found to be major contributors to adolescent burnout. Remember, it doesn't matter if the pressure is real; it is only important that you *perceive* it as real, for real or not, the pressure cooker some of you live within can be deadly.

- *Excessive academic competition*—I've heard seventh and eighth graders brag to me about staying up all night to study for an exam. I've listened to countless stories of kids who get ill before exams, experience violent migraine headaches before the school year begins, and who have to get totally "wasted" to come down off the week's anxiety high. The stress surrounding SAT results is "nuclear" in some schools. Ripe for burnout!

- *Excessive athletic competition*—Watch the parents at a high school game and you would think the fate of the world was hanging in the balance. It is unbelievable the pressure some adolescent athletes are under to win, to produce championships, to earn fame and the fortune of scholarships. Ripe for burnout!

- *Excessive pressure to be a winner*—Many teens are absolutely obsessed by the need for the right look, the right friends, the right grades, going into the right college, getting the right job, earning the right kind of money. You will sacrifice anything, including physical, emotional, and spiritual health, to get it. Ripe for burnout!

- *No time to play*—I've heard some teens describe a calendar so jammed there is literally no time to relax, to take a walk, to just think, to fool around, to pray, to dream, or to love. Ripe for burnout!

- *No real friends*—When everyone becomes your academic or athletic or social "opponent," you begin to keep people at arm's length. Climbing the ladder of success often means keeping your rung clear of competion. Watching out for #1, the philosophy often required to be a winner, seldom allows for closeness of any kind. Ripe for burnout!

One thing you need to understand about being human is this: we all have a reservoir of coping ability, a supply of inner strength that is used to grapple with the very real, and very common, struggles of life. Humans often mistakenly believe that there is some magical underground spring which constantly replenishes this reservoir, but we are wrong. When you're out, you're out. I've learned, as so many other adults have and so many of you will or already have, that we human beings can "drain dry," physically, emotionally, and spiritually. If burnout is not to be an issue in your life, with all of its potentially dangerous consequences, you will have to learn how to maintain your reservoir and keep your level of coping ability relatively high. The goal of the next section is to help you learn how to fill up your reservoir, and to do so requires the source of all true inner strength—Jesus Christ.

Expect droughts

> The words of the Teacher, son of David, king in Jerusalem:
>
> "Meaningless! Meaningless!"
> says the Teacher.
> "Utterly meaningless!
> Everything is meaningless."
> What does man gain from all his labor
> at which he toils under the sun?
>
> ....
>
> All things are wearisome,
> more than one can say.
> The eye never has enough of seeing,
> or the ear its fill of hearing.
> What has been will be again,
> what has been done will be done again;
> there is nothing new under the sun.
>
> (Eccles. 1:1-3, 8-19)

During my last year of ministry in Milwaukee I preached on the above biblical text five times. I can't consciously recall my reasons for choosing this passage so often, but I am confident that it was no coincidence. It was in that final year that I felt most burned out, and I believe that my choice of this text reflected my spiritual state. I found comfort in the fact that the Teacher in Ecclesiastes seemed to be suffering from burnout too.

Human beings derive comfort from knowing we are not alone—even in our suffering. For me, the knowledge that a biblical author could relate to my condition was a real source of support. And for those three faces from my youth group, the knowledge that they weren't alone helped make being burned out far less frightening. It is crucial for us humans to not feel isolated or alone. I guess that's why solitary confinement is often used as a form of punishment.

If you are feeling drained dry—exhausted by the demands of school, athletics, clubs, friends, parents—or under terrible stress from trying to get into that right group or that right school or worn out from the endless competition over grades, teams, dates, popularity, appearance, and limp from the constant worry over the future, SATs, the job market, sexual choices, drug choices—remember *you are not alone.* There are many of you who are worn down, burned out, and burned up by life itself. Even the passage from Ecclesiastes witnesses to that fact. But it serves as a biblical reminder that you are understood by God as well.

You will experience these dry periods throughout your life, but they are never more difficult to handle than as an adolescent. It is probably not hard for you to draw the connection between the young person who is exhausted physically, emotionally, and especially spiritually, and the young person who might seriously consider suicide. They are fairly often one and the same. However, if you expect some difficult stretches in life, and you prepare for times when all enthusiasm seems gone, those times will not be nearly as frightening—or *potentially deadly.* And if you also know you are not alone or strange or crazy to feel as you do, the fear of these drained periods will disappear.

I'm glad that Ecclesiastes was included in Scripture,

for I feel so much more normal every time I read it. Take some time yourself to read this brief book in the Bible, and you too will know that God understands burnout and that there is always light at the end of the tunnel. That bright light for us as Christians is Jesus himself, and that promise of his presence can guide us to the end of any tunnel we might have to crawl through in life—even burnout.

Chosen aloneness

> Very early in the morning, while it was still dark, Jesus got up, left the house and went off to a solitary place, where he prayed. Simon and his companions went to look for him, and when they found him, they exclaimed: "Everyone is looking for you!"
>
> Jesus replied, "Let us go somewhere else—to the nearby villages—so I can preach there also. That is why I have come." So he traveled throughout Galilee, preaching in their synagogues and driving out demons.
>
> (Mark 1:35-39)

Even Jesus needed to pull back, to break away and to get his act back together. Even Jesus needed *to fill up his reservoir.* We all need time alone, time when we choose to be still and silent, time when we just need to figure out what is happening to us. You will find it of great benefit to just take some time alone and ask yourself how you are doing. This is never more important than when you are feeling burned out, for during those dry times we need to water ourselves with some awareness. Here are some questions to promote thinking and feeling, and more importantly, to offer clarity, focus, and strategies for filling up your reservoir:

1. How do you reward yourself for a job well done?
2. Are you satisfied with your best effort or are you never satisfied?
3. Do you worry a great deal over things you can't control?
4. What do you need from your friends, or parents, or even God?
5. What people make you feel at peace or most at ease with being yourself? How much time do you spend with them?
6. Do you spend considerable time with some people who always make you feel lousy or who act artificial?
7. Are you your own worst critic? Are you fair with your self? Are you forgiving of your self?
8. When was the last time you really prayed? really worshiped?
9. What changes do you really need to make in your self, in your life-style?
10. Do you let people love you? Do you feel unlovable? Why?

It is so vital for you to learn how to take that long walk, to sit quietly by the water or under a tree, to gaze at the stars or a sunrise, or to just lie in bed without music or magazines or anything other than your self. You need that kind of chosen alone time, as we all do, in order to refuel your own spirit, and to let the Holy Spirit do some filling of your reservoir as well. The time we do choose to be alone is often the only time we might also be slow enough, silent enough, still enough, and open enough to let the Spirit in. When we finally just shut up and listen to our inner self, our true self, our heart of hearts, our conscience, we often hear the Word of God as well.

> In the same way, the Spirit helps us in our weakness. We do not know what we ought to pray for, but the Spirit himself intercedes for us with groans that words cannot express. And he who searches our hearts knows the mind of the Spirit, because the Spirit intercedes for the saints in accordance with God's will.
>
> (Rom. 8:26-27)

Jump!

> "Come to me, all you who are weary and burdened, and I will give you rest. Take my yoke upon you and learn from me, for I am gentle and humble in heart, and you will find rest for your souls. For my yoke is easy and my burden is light."
>
> (Matt. 11:28-30)

I remember the first time I heard the slogan, "Let go, let God." I liked the sound, but I hated the content. I think surrendering ourselves to God is so tough because we associate surrender with being a white-flag-waving *loser.* The idea of saying, "OK, I can't handle this anymore—it's all yours, God," just goes against our need to always be in control. All I can tell you is that surrender is a giant leap of faith.

When you are burned out you're like the child who stands on the top step of the porch. Somehow, you know that the father who is yelling for you to jump into his arms is worth trusting, but you are momentarily frozen. Finally, with no place left to go, you rock back and forth, throw your arms forward, and leap into the air. With a mouth wide open with hope and fear, you fall into your father's waiting arms. What do you do next? You run back up to the top step and do it again . . . and again . . . and again. Surrender, like a child's top step leap, is risky at first, but once you learn to trust the arms below, it becomes as natural as breathing. I can't tell you or teach you to trust. I can only *ask* you to trust Christ's ability to catch your burdens, and to embrace your burnout with the arms of love and hope. Jesus waits, and in a way, he calls all day, every day, to all of us, "Jump!"

What will you get for your efforts? What rewards will you receive for taking the risk of jumping? The rewards are the brains to know how to keep your reservoir full, the heart to hope and to keep on loving, the courage to pick up your cross and follow Christ, and the reward of coming home to your self and to your God. God gives us a burden we can handle easily, the burden of being exactly, and only, who God created you to be.

So, if you are burned out and wondering why bother taking this "life-exam" that everyone appears to fail, I beg you to jump, because if you do, you will find that life with Christ is an exam everyone can pass with ease! Why? Because Jesus has already given us all the answers—in the front, and the middle, and the back of the Book!

6 "WHAT'S THE BIG DEAL ABOUT SUICIDE, IF I FEEL DEAD ALREADY?"

Sometimes during my workshops with young people, I use a gimmick to make a point. One point I often try to make is that sometimes humans choose to feel dead or to deaden themselves. Don't close this book! I'm not nuts! Let me explain by sharing with you the gimmick that I use. It should help you understand what I mean.

At a carefully selected point toward the beginning of a workshop, I will ask the group to describe for me what it feels like to be drunk, stoned, wasted, buzzed. I admit that at first there are some awkward smiles and giggles and groans, but gradually I get some response. The responses I get almost always go something like this:

"No worries, no tension."

"On top of the world."
"A little bit like God."
"Totally calm and at peace."
"All the hassles are over."

At another carefully chosen time, but much later in the workshop, I will ask the same group "What do you think it would feel like to be dead?" Again, after some awkwardness and hesitation, the responses start to flow, and they usually go something like this:

"No worries, no tension."
"On top of the world."
"A little bit like God."
"Totally calm and at peace."
"All the hassles are over."

Since I tape almost every workshop I conduct, I will at this point play back for the group their earlier responses concerning being drunk or using chemicals of some kind. The kids are quite shocked at the obvious similarity between what they think death might be like, and what they might already know being high to be. The young people are able to understand how a human being can actually choose to feel dead, or to deaden oneself, as one might do with drinking or drugs.

Choosing to feel dead is like choosing to live like a robot. Robots, though fascinating pieces of machinery and technology, are still not alive in any way, shape, or form. Therefore, to choose to live as a robot is to choose to stop doing or being all the things which make us human, which make us alive:

1. Stop feeling.
2. Stop thinking seriously about anything.

3. Stop being creative.
4. Stop dreaming.
5. Stop being curious.
6. Stop using your imagination.
7. Stop loving.
8. Stop hoping.
9. Stop changing.
10. Stop learning.
11. Stop praying or worshiping.
12. Stop taking any risks, or fighting for what you believe in.

There are some of you who, in an effort to look cool, calm, and collected (life on a deodorant commercial), choose simply to live like a robot. By stopping all those experiences that make you feel alive, you also avoid all the pain and conflict that goes with "aliveness." For still others of you, it is that very pain that you feel has forced you to stop.

It may seem impossible to stop feeling alive, but I think you know that some of you are getting to be experts at it. Maybe you put all your energies into your grades, your romance, your sport, your music, or whatever, but often the goal is the same, to be free from all the other emotions and experiences that make you alive and make life such a wonderful challenge. Many of you are happiest when you feel the least. You seldom think seriously about anything. You believe in little to nothing. You have no dreams. And that, my friends, is what I mean by feeling dead.

Without question, in my experience with suicidal adolescents, the most common comment I have heard is, "What's the big deal about suicide, if I feel dead already?" It seems to me the strongest warning sign for young people who are becoming depressed or suicidal is when they choose to feel dead more and more often. The way you can tell if a friend, or brother, or sister, or even yourself, is headed for some potentially deep trouble, is to be aware of how often the person is choosing to avoid feeling fully alive. When you see somebody consistently avoiding reality, escaping into some fantasy world, or acting as if they are "feelingless," "unhurtable," or just plain "out of it," you are probably receiving a warning signal that someone is in trouble.

Conformity

We all want to fit in to some degree. We all do our fair share of conforming. We all enjoy pleasing certain people—friends, parents, teachers, coaches, ministers, or even a favorite neighbor or relative—and so we try to meet their expectations of us. Conformity for teenagers is probably most obvious in terms of what is considered fashionable when it comes to clothes, music, television shows or movies, sports, foods, hairstyles, even college choices. You want to be fashionable. Your image is important.

There is really nothing wrong with the fact that we humans worry about fitting in, and that at times we choose to go with the flow of the crowd. However, there are times when choosing to conform can become a real deadening experience, and those are the times when you feel like you are sacrificing your soul to fit in. I have recorded the comments of some young people who found they were conforming too often and too much, and giving up too much in the process. By reflecting on what these youths have said, I hope you can see how and when conformity can become dangerous:

- "My group was it. They chose my clothes, my friends, and which classes I took. I smoked dope to fit in. I even slept with one guy just to win their approval."

- "My parents always wanted me to be a doctor. My dad is one. I hate science though, and I love music and art. I went to the college they wanted, took the courses they wanted, and got the grades they wanted, for the first year at least. My sophomore year I flunked out. I just don't want to be a doctor. I want to go into film, or into some area where I can use my music."

- "I lost my best friend in the whole world, just because my other friends thought he was weird. All they really meant was that he wasn't a jock."

- "I am so sick of getting drunk every weekend. It's boring. I just do it because everyone else in my crowd loves to party."

- "My boyfriend asked me what I really wanted out of life. I had no idea. All my life I've just done what others want. I've never once asked me what I want."

- "I dropped out of youth group because, well, my friends think it's for sissies and stuff."

Conformity is normal, but you choose to be a robot if you let other people determine who you like and love, what your morals will be, or even your dreams. To be influenced by the crowd is one thing, but to let the crowd take away your unique God-given beliefs and feelings is another. If you let others, even well-intentioned parents, *dictate* (as in *dictator*) what you think, how you look, how you act, even your ethical choices, you have sacrificed too much. It may be far easier for you to follow the crowd or the wishes of others, but in the end you may have lost the greatest gift of all—your self. Crowds can make us feel accepted, affirmed, and comfortable, but they should never ask us to give up our own feelings, thoughts, attitudes, and beliefs, in order to fit in. Anytime you sacrifice your unique self to the wishes of the group, you are choosing to be a robot, and that is one sure way to feel dead, in fact, spiritually to be dead.

More on chemicals

The use of alcohol and drugs is widespread, and I have to admit it is a huge part of the American lifestyle. I seldom go to anyone's house where I am not offered a drink within 15 minutes of being there. I can hardly remember attending a party of any kind that did not feature alcohol. Simply put, we live in a world that is fascinated with, and often addicted to, alcohol and other drugs.

Chemicals continue to be a popular means of feeling dead, and no matter how accepted it is, the use of chemicals continues to have potentially deadly consequences. I have heard many young people tell me that they drink because they like the taste. Well, I like the taste of Pepsi, but I don't drink seven or eight bottles in a row. People drink and do drugs primarily to get high, and ironically that high is a feeling of being at peace, or better put, dead—life's ultimate low. "Rest in peace" is a funeral slogan. It is also the goal of getting drunk or stoned or high. Like it or not, if you are really honest, you use drugs—alcohol included—to get away from it all. What you are getting away from is life, being human, being alive. Chemicals provide instant deadness, like an anesthetic a dentist might use, only this time it is applied to your spirit.

The following list tells you when chemicals are gaining control of your life. They spell deadly consequences.

1. When you feel you must use a chemical to deal with every worry, problem, or fear.
2. When you have to use a chemical in order to socialize or relax.
3. When your use of chemicals makes your sexual choices for you.
4. When you use chemicals and an automobile at the same time.
5. When you are never happy without using chemicals.
6. When chemicals are always on your mind.
7. When you can't imagine life without chemicals.
8. When you spend more time with chemicals than with Christ.
9. When you choose friends only if they use chemicals too.
10. When your recreation time almost always includes getting "wrecked."

I am often asked if chemicals cause teen suicide. In my mind, chemicals are the doorman to suicidal thoughts; they invite you in. I have never counseled a suicidal youth who didn't get involved to some degree with chemicals. To me, chemicals are a cause, a real force that contributes to the staggering rate of teen suicide in this country.

Our world

Can you imagine taking Jesus to see a movie like *The Texas Chainsaw Massacre, Halloween, Rambo, Friday the 13th,* or *The Terminator,* and explaining to him that this is *entertainment?* Can you explain why so many young people are so interested and heavily invested in things like Ninja and the martial arts? We live in a very violent world, and I fear that many of you are so numb to that violence and bloodshed that nothing will shock you. In other words, you are dead to death, or at least death is so commonplace that it has even become a means of entertainment.

Today's Hollywood horror film is aimed at you, but it really isn't a horror film anymore. Horror films had a plot, a climax, a moment of great terror where everyone screamed, and then a winding down. Today's teenage horror movie is always the same. Several young, innocent kids gather at a camp or a house or a ski chalet for some kind of party, and by the end of the movie they have all been grotesquely destroyed. Wise, middle-aged Murphy, the lead character in the film *Murphy's Romance,* walks out of such a film and he explains his departure with the words, "I worked one summer in a slaughter house, I don't need to pay to watch it on the screen." For me, it is films such as these that are real signs of deadness in our world and within today's adolescent population. One young woman remarked to me, "Sometimes I go to those stupid movies just to see if I can still feel anything. I mean, the whole point of the film is to find new ways to shock us or to gross us out. So I go. I want to see if they can make me scream. Most of the time though, I just laugh at all the blood and gore. I don't feel a thing."

We live in a world that sometimes encourages us to live like robots, to feel dead, or to be content to live life in such a shallow way that we may never really know the joy of being fully and honestly alive. It is my belief that faith in Jesus Christ requires us to live as human beings, not robots, and to love the experience of *being alive to the fullest*. We must avoid at all costs choosing to feel dead.

It's OK to be human

For several years a very prominent businessman came in for counseling with me. He came primarily because he just never felt happy or content. One day he came in for his appointment, looking extremely nervous. I asked him why he was so jittery, and he said, "Well, I just did something stupid, and I hope nobody saw." I asked him if he felt comfortable sharing with me what he had done. He told me that he had spent two full hours that morning just sitting at the end of a pier overlooking Lake Michigan.

I was confused, and I had a hard time not laughing. I asked him, "What on earth was so stupid about that?" He explained to me that he was terrified that someone might have seen him. Again I asked, "So what?" He again explained that he just didn't want anyone at the bank, where he was president, to see him wasting so much time or "thinking I was about to kill myself."

This incident was a real breakthrough in our counseling. I finally realized how driven this man was to function like a robot. We spent months together trying to get him to give himself permission to just be human—to take walks, ride a bike, play with his children, see a movie, or sit at the end of a pier for a whole day if he chose. I had to remind him that he was never meant to be a machine that never stopped working. I believe he finally did learn that he had the right to take time to feel, think, pray, meditate, and play, and that he need not be embarrassed when his humanness showed. I still find it incredible to think how consumed this man was in the belief that he had to turn off all his human needs and function as a smoothly running robot who works, works, works. Now that was a waste of time!

Human beings are created in the image of God. Robots are created in the image of the imperfect human. Since we are created in the image of God, we are created in the spirit of Jesus Christ, a spirit who chose to celebrate life and humanness. Jesus wept at the death of his friend Lazarus. His anger went out of control when he confronted the money-changers—rip-off artists—at the temple doors. He surrounded himself with friends he needed and wanted, as life is never meant to be spent in isolation. Jesus attended a wedding or two, and those were some big parties. He loved—without any concern for how things looked to others—poor people, prostitutes, people with leprosy, tax collectors, and those who were outcast and brokenhearted. Jesus doubted; he, too, asked why God had abandoned him. Jesus even asked God to remove the rock of death from his path, just as we all do, or will do (Luke 22:42). Jesus was tempted (Luke 4:1-13). He knew how to laugh, and he prayed and hoped and dreamed, just like us. We are created in the image of a Christ who did not reject his humanness, but embraced it as a marvelous gift. Jesus did not find humanness a curse to be endured, but a blessing to be celebrated.

Though a robot may appear to be together, self-sufficient, competent, and in control, there is something missing. What's missing is that which makes us human—the capacity to feel deeply, to think seriously, and to believe intensely. Robots cannot love anyone as they love themselves, nor can they love their God with their whole heart. If you choose to live like a robot, you will have sacrificed the human spirit granted you by Christ. No matter how tough being a plain old human being can be, it sure beats being a feelingless and faithless machine.

Wally and the thief

Therefore Jesus said again, "I tell you the truth, I am the gate for the sheep. All who ever came before me were thieves and robbers, but the sheep did not listen to them. I am the gate; whoever enters through me will be saved. He will come in and go out, and find pasture. The thief comes only to steal and kill and destroy; I have come that they may have life, and have it to the full."

(John 10:7-10)

Wally wasn't a bad kid, he was a mad kid. He always dressed tough, talked tough, and made sure all of his actions were appropriately macho. Those of us who knew him well, knew he was a grizzly bear on the outside, but a teddy bear inside. Wally had developed a bad drinking problem. Though he was one of the finest athletes in the school, he had all but dropped out of school sports. Though he was quite bright, every semester he just barely scraped by. He had several encounters with the police, some for vandalism, and of course, drunk driving.

Wally seldom talked, but when he did, and when he was sober, he was brutally honest. He had asked me to go for a ride, not wanting anyone to see him at my office. We drove for three hours, and Wally did most of the talking. He told me that he knew he was an alcoholic, and that his father was too, and that he thought his life was going down the same dead end as his dad's. "He was a big jock, good student, popular, and now look at him. He's a drunk. He drives a truck when he can get himself sober enough. He comes home, drinks, and falls asleep by 8:00 every night. My mother just watches him and cries all the time."

I asked Wally if he thought he could change, or if he even wanted to. He told me that though he did want to change, he felt as if he'd lost all his dreams already. As he stared out the window he sadly said, "There's just not much left in me. I feel so empty, so alone. I feel like my dreams died, like I just lost out on growing up, on learning how to handle things.

While all the other kids were learning to face their problems, I just got drunk. I really feel like I've already killed everything that was ever good about me."

We continued to talk, and of course, I tried to convince Wally that it wasn't too late, that he wasn't dead yet, though admittedly he had made a lot of dead choices. As we drove into the church parking lot, Wally turned and stared into my eyes, and spoke with both anger and pain, "I thought I had found the good life, Pastor Bill. What a joke. I thought I had this real cool image—mean, macho, and never a wimp. I could even tempt death. You know, drive fast, drive drunk, swallow a few too many pills with my beer. I'm killing me, man, I'm killing me. Do you know what? I know God had better things in mind for me than this, I know he did."

I had never ever heard Wally say a thing about God before, but Wally was sure on target with this comment. God sure did have better things in mind for Wally. Jesus Christ never wanted Wally's life to be stolen by a thief like booze. He never wanted to see such a talented young man so hollow and so hopeless. Jesus never wanted to see so many gifts wasted, so much precious time destroyed. Jesus wanted an abundant life for Wally. So did I, and so did many friends Wally never knew he had—teachers, coaches, neighbors, and kids he never spoke to in school. Wally died in a drunk driving accident three months after our conversation. I know Jesus wept. So did I.

Jesus wants you to have a full life. A life full of questions that will make you grow. A life full of friends that will let you know the joy of intimacy. A life full of dreams that will challenge you to discipline your God-given talents. A life full of faith that will help you discover your place in God's kingdom. A life full of love that will inspire you to create new hope. Jesus never intended for us to find escaping life more pleasurable than living it, and he never would want us to give up our souls to the thief of relief, relief from the crosses he has given us to pick up and carry.

Becoming

> He who was seated on the throne said, "I am making everything new!" Then he said, "Write this down, for these words are trustworthy and true."
>
> (Rev. 21:5)

At times you may find yourself hopelessly caught in a rut. You feel like you are just marching in place—in quicksand. At these times, the temptation to choose deadness seems like no big deal. I mean, who cares if you just follow the crowd or get stoned whenever you feel the urge, or just choose to ignore what you are feeling. The same stupid world will still be there when you get back to reality. It is at times when you feel like your entire life is a big rerun that the temptation to just numb yourself grows more intense. It is also at these times that you must remember that Jesus gives you the strength to change, to grow, to deepen, and to mature, for you are never finished, but *always becoming*.

Think of it this way: You are always granted a fresh start. You are always being forgiven. The Holy Spirit is always giving you ways to improve. You are promised that God will be with you always, and that God will assist you in becoming the disciple you were created to be. God gives you a forever promise, and that promise guarantees you a life of love and fulfillment, whenever you are willing to receive the ongoing love of God. You are never really old in spirit, and staleness is a state of mind. With Jesus Christ you can experience each day as another opportunity to become your dreams.

When I was in therapy, my therapist asked me to fill out what he called "prescription cards," anytime I felt good, had a good idea, had a good day, or could feel myself making a wise choice or handling a situation maturely. At first I thought the idea was a waste of time. He told me to tape the cards to the mirror on my dresser, and since I was paying him good money, I decided to do just that. After a month, I could no longer see myself—my mirror was covered with cards. As I looked at the growing collection of cards, I felt as if I were looking into the face of Christ, and that face was telling me how many good things happen every day. I realized how many good things in life are never noticed or too soon forgotten, and I saw how much I was learning and maturing all of the time and just how blessed I was by a God who both comforts me and challenges me to grow. If you look into the face of Christ, even if it is created out of a pack of prescription cards, you, too, will soon see in his eyes the reflection of a beautiful, brand-new you. Staring into the face of Christ, you see a self that is wonderfully becoming, a self that is growing in pain, learning in worry, and maturing with anxiety, but a self that knows the miracle of just being alive.

7

"WILL THERE BE A WORLD TO LIVE IN WHEN I'M 30?"

I know there are many adults who will tell you that times have always been tough and the issues of your world are no worse or more difficult to face than they were for any other teenager of any other time. I disagree. I am not in the position to say that you are facing the toughest issues or the toughest times of all time, but I am certain that it is harder for you to face the realities of your world than it was for me to face those of mine. These are exceptionally tough, complex, and often terrifying times, and your task of becoming a happy, healthy, well-educated adult is much more difficult than it was for me.

My conclusion—that emotionally and spiritually you have it tougher than I did—is well supported by the fears I hear you so often talking about, joking about, and even praying about. I've listened to your fears in counseling sessions and discussion groups, I've provoked them in workshops and seminars and retreats, and I've read about them in your stories, term papers, and journals. Your fears are much more intense and real for you than any I can remember from my adolescent years. The following list consists of fears I have heard expressed by young people over the last few years. The list contains worries which pose a far more serious, far more genuine threat to your future, than the worries I recall grappling with as a youth.

1. The fear of purchasing a product that has been tampered with, such as Tylenol laced with cyanide.
2. The fear of experiencing violent crime, especially murders for sport, or becoming a statistic of a serial murderer.
3. The fear of being taken hostage or kidnapped.
4. The fear of a terrorist bombing.
5. The fear of a nuclear accident like Chernobyl or Three Mile Island.
6. The fear of being slipped a bad drug at a party, or as a prank.
7. The fear of a nuclear war. (I worried about the *possibility* of a war; many of you see such a war as a *certainty*.)
8. The fear of carcinogens being present in products, foods, and pollutants.
9. The fear of running out of natural resources.
10. The fear of the breakdown of the ozone layer.
11. The fear of AIDS.
12. The fear of being swept into a cult.

The above list is just a sampling of the kinds of very real and terrifying fears you live with every day.

Though many adults, including many of your parents, would like to believe you are not dealing with such issues or fears, I am convinced that you are and that you want adults to recognize that these fears are a part of your daily reality. Though I am not thrilled to have composed such a list of fears for today's youth, I know in my heart that you find the list far less frightening than the tendency of adults to avoid the issue. I also share this list with you because I believe as Christians we can do something about these fears. As followers of Jesus we can find the strength not just to cope, but to overcome our fears in order to build a liveable future.

Reread the list of fears. You'll notice they have one thing in common: they all deal with situations over which you basically have *no control.* How do you know if a product has been tampered with or your food has been sprayed with a pesticide loaded with cancer-causing agents? Can you predict when a nuclear reactor will go into meltdown or whether a flock of geese will confuse the computer into thinking they are in fact incoming Soviet missiles, causing the nuclear war dominos to fall? In all honesty, you and I have little *direct* control over such potentially destructive situations, and that only heightens our fear. You aren't making these fears up. You aren't being too emotional. Your fears are real. The fear of being the innocent victim, of having no control over the situation, is normal! We can never escape our fears by pretending they don't exist, and adults who pretend that today's youth are too innocent to have them are only making matters worse. Fear, no matter how terrifying, must be faced.

However, fear over matters which are out of your direct control are the toughest to face, because these fears are just so huge, so complex, so like mercury—always moving and impossible to grasp.

The kinds of fears I have shared with you certainly make your world an *anxious* one, for anxiety is really the experience of uncertainty, of not knowing what to expect next. The range of fears I see you experiencing obviously produces a great degree of stress, while at the same time it breaks down your trust, your hope, your dreams, and for some of you, your faith. The level of fear in today's youth is extraordinarily high, and it is gradually eroding one's belief in self, the world, and life itself.

While working and being with young people, I have observed the following three reactions to living in a frightening world, a world in which many of you honestly often ask, "Will there be a world to live in when I'm 30?":

1. Living totally for the moment, almost as if there will be no tomorrow. This kind of living for the moment *only* is dominated by the accumulation of things, and a philosophy of life best expressed as, "I want to have it all." Unfortunately, the *all* is seen only as material things.
2. Reckless living, living without ethics or morals, and living out a philosophy of life that has two major beliefs, "If it feels good, do it!" and "I'm not hurting anybody but myself, so it's OK." The sad part of this attitude is not only that it is "me-centered" but that it ironically shows no love for that "me" at all.

The one who over-indulges in chemicals, takes unnecessary risks while driving or partying or whatever, and seems to enjoy tempting death, really shows a total lack of respect for self.

3. Living without hope or faith, and viewing life as something to be gotten through. This philosophy of life is simply, "Who cares?" and reflects a basic belief that the only way to endure life is to become a cynic. If I don't care, I won't worry.

Though most of you don't reflect any particular one of these reactions, I would guess that all of you can relate to each in some way. Some of you, however, will see yourselves immediately in one of these three brief descriptions. If you do, I hope you realize the powerful impact that our shared times, our shared world, our shared fears can have on your own life. You are not alone! It is fair to say that if you do find yourself in one of these three areas, living out one of these three philosophies of life, you have probably considered the possibility of suicide. I say this because these philosophies are slow suicide themselves, asking you to give up on all that really matters, all that is of real value to life and to Jesus. The question, "Will there be a world to live in when I'm 30?" is slow suicide if it is asked without faith or without a basic belief in the power of God.

I want to share with you how I feel Jesus responds to your times, to your fears, to slow suicides and warped philosophies of life, and to the whole issue of the fate of the world. I believe that Jesus can create the courage needed to make tomorrow worth the wait, the future a vision of bright hope.

Holding your breath

> "There will be signs in the sun, moon and stars. On the earth, nations will be in anguish and perplexity at the roaring and tossing of the sea. Men will faint from terror, apprehensive of what is coming on the world, for the heavenly bodies will be shaken. At that time they will see the Son of Man coming in a cloud with power and great glory."
>
> (Luke 21:25-27)

Throughout history there have been times when the world has held its breath in fearful waiting, wondering if "the end" was on the horizon. I know that this doesn't lessen your fear, but by remembering that fear, even terror, has always been with the human race, you can keep your fear in perspective.

I recall standing before the locker room doors leading onto the football field, and holding my breath to try and clear out the butterflies in my stomach. Somehow, even if it is for just a moment, holding your breath can relax you. When I am feeling overwhelmed, which often happens after viewing the six o'clock news, I will hold my breath and recite the Lord's Prayer. At first I felt guilty using the Lord's Prayer in such a gimmicky way, but now I believe it is a good way to put things back in perspective. The Lord's Prayer reminds me that the world is God's, and that all I can do is to trust that God will be true to his covenant with us, and that God is in control. All I can do is to have a faith that God's will can be done, that God's kingdom can be built, and that I can help only by trusting fully in that promise.

Making your peace

Blessed are the peacemakers,
for they will be called sons of God.

(Matt. 5:9)

One summer, my buddies and I hit four new wiffle balls into the Patterson's backyard, and they kept all four. Just before school was to begin—our first year in junior high—we decided to get even with the Pattersons. We made several phone orders, four to the Chicken Jamborees around town, two to the Pugh Coal Company, and three to diaper services. We asked for their delivery trucks—Chicken Jamboree had station wagons with a large chicken attached to the top, it even had flashing lights for eyes—to all arrive at six o'clock in the evening. They did. We five guys watched from my front porch as the Patterson's driveway suddenly looked like an expressway traffic jam. Mrs. Patterson looked over at the five innocent faces on the porch, and she screamed, "I know you did it! I know who it was! Wait until your parents hear!"

My parents heard. I had to help pay back everything we had ordered. I was grounded for the first month of school, including the opening dance. However, the worst part was that Mr. and Mrs. Patterson stopped speaking to my parents. For the entire time we had lived there, they had been my folks' very best friends. They shared picnics together, movies, baseball games at the park down the block, and just sitting out on the front porch for evening conversation. My shame was overwhelming as I watched Mrs. Patterson walk by my mother at the grocery store, or saw my father and Mr. Patterson silently cutting their lawns, with the picket fence as sort of a Berlin Wall between them.

I will never forget the night Mrs. Patterson showed up at the back door. She was carrying Christmas cookies, and she said to my mom, "It's Christmas, Hedy, and I just couldn't go through one more day without my best friend." They both cried and hugged, and of course, I left the room. The very next day Mr. Patterson came over to watch "The Honeymooners" with my dad. My prayers were answered. It was over. I was forgiven. Peace between the Pattersons and Grimbols reigned again. That Christmas I got a gift from the Pattersons, something that never happened before. I opened it hurriedly, and inside was a case of 12 wiffle balls. We all laughed. I can't ever remember a laugh feeling that good.

What happens at Christmas? What makes it a season of the ceasefire? Well, we all know that it is much more than the tinsel and all the glittering trimmings, much more than the gobs of gifts, although all of that can be a way of expressing love and joy and specialness. Still, in our heart of hearts we know that a deeper truth of Christmas is the melting of frozen hearts, and I would add, frozen faiths. At Christmas we greet strangers with "Merry Christmas." We give generously to the poor. Charity and welfare are seen as healthy and natural, not as freeloading or rip-offs. Members of families quit pouting and renew old bonds again. Friends forgive and forget. We worship and pray and sing with enthusiasm. We gather over meals filled with thanksgiving. We cry and hug and laugh a lot. We get goosebumps over the silliest things, like watching the scrawny tree evolve into a decorated masterpiece. And we become like children, excited about everything.

At Christmas we often become the people we were created to be: people who are merciful, people who are just and people who care and share and dare to love. At Christmas we tend to make our peace at home, at school, at work, on the team, in the club, within the neighborhood, around town, even with our world and ourselves. At Christmas the world gets rid of rankings, and everyone is seen as a winner, everyone is on top for awhile. Is there any reason why we make our peace only at Christmas? No, there is no real reason, other than to be a peacemaker is risky, and it requires a lot of courage and a lot of faith in Jesus Christ. And at Christmas our thoughts are drawn back to that Savior of the world, born in a manger.

If you really want to get rid of the terror of your world, maybe you can begin by putting the Christmas spirit into all your days. You may not be able to erase the fears of your times, but you can create a bit of peace within your family, school, with an enemy, with Jesus Christ, and with your self. If you can put the Christmas spirit into the center of your hearts and your days, you may not eliminate the terror of your world, but you will strengthen your faith and deepen your relationship with Jesus. When your faith is firmer you will be able to face your world, armed with a defiant hope and ready to do battle. A little Christmas right this very minute will help you get over your fear of being in a broken world.

Faithing your future

> The people walking in darkness
>   have seen a great light;
> on those living in the land of the shadow of death
>   a light has dawned.
>
> ....
>
> For to us a child is born,
>   to us a son is given,
>   and the government will be on his shoulders.
> And he will be called
>   Wonderful Counselor, Mighty God,
>   Everlasting Father, Prince of Peace.
>
> (Isa. 9:2, 6)

I have good friends who tell a true story about arriving late at a theater and then being ushered into a pitch black chamber that is used for soundproofing. With almost 10 yards between the entrance doors and the next set of doors that would let them into the theater itself, this quartet of folks were left in total darkness, groping their way along the walls, trying to locate that next set of doors. As they shuffled along with their hands to the walls, they started to giggle. On stage a shotgun blast went off. Without hesitation, and for no known reason, one member of the lost party cried out, "I've been shot!" Needless to say the four of them became a lump of laughter sitting on the floor of that dark, soundproofing tunnel. When they finally did manage to gather the strength and courage to enter the theater, the last 10 rows of the audience were all clutching their stomachs in laughter and muttering, "They are the ones who thought they got shot."

I have heard my friends tell this story often—obviously it is worthy of repeating if laughter is desired—and each time someone will also make the insightful comment, "It is sort of sad to be living in a world where the first thing you think of, even in a theater, is that the shot was meant for you!" It is sad. It is unfortunate. We do, however, live in a land of deep darkness, and we are a people who have walked in darkness. The terror of our times is real for us all, especially for you, the youth who inherit this world and this darkness. Like the people of which the Scripture speaks, we are no strangers to darkness, and we know that frightening feeling of being lost in blackness.

Still, again like the Scripture says, we are a people who have seen a great light. We must live as people who believe in that light, who follow that light, and who spread that light like the arrival of a dawn. If we face the future with that light as our guide, then we will walk with steps of hope and assurance that we will find our way out of the darkness. If you believe in the truth of Christmas, that for us a child is born and a Son given, and that all governing rests now upon his shoulders, and that he is the Prince of Peace, then you have received a light that can defeat the darkness.

Faithing the future means only realizing that without faith we become trapped in darkness. Without faith the future looks gloomy and bleak. Without faith in Jesus Christ the answer to the question, "Will there be a world to live in when I'm 30?" is a resounding *no*. It is faith in Jesus that not only keeps you going, but helps you locate your own dreams and your own ability to be a disciple. I really believe that if you have come to the point where your future looks like one giant nightmare of darkness, then the only option left, the only option I see as worthy of trying, is building a stronger faith in Jesus Christ. Jesus is the light at the end of the tunnel. He is the source of the strength needed to face our fears, tame the terror, and faith the future. Jesus Christ is the Light of the world, and we are called to soak in these rays, as well as to radiate their warmth.

Is this just too easy an answer? No, not really, for it is an answer that does not pretend that the night will disappear, but only promises that a new day will dawn. Jesus is an answer, but never an easy one. Jesus simply tells you that if you follow him, you will be following someone who preaches good news to poor people, proclaims liberty for those who are oppressed, binds the broken hearts of lonely and lost ones, feeds those who are hungry, and clothes those who are naked. If we follow Jesus, we will not only become part of the rising sun of hope, but we will have no time to be swallowed whole with fear. The terror of our times is eased and at times even erased by living the discipline of a disciple.

8

"CAN I HONESTLY HOPE TO MAKE A DIFFERENCE?"

"Why don't you think you can make a difference?"

"Everything is so huge. The problems are so big. I'm just one little person."

"It might be a small difference, but it's still a difference."

"I know, but why bother trying when the problems are so endless. We'll never have enough food for the hungry. Plus, why care when nobody else does?"

"I have to admit that a lot of people don't seem to care, but I've always respected you for being one young person who did."

"Yeah, but that's why I'm thought of as a 'goodie two shoes.'"

"You mean just because you care about people and the world, you're accused of being overly religious?"

"If I said I wanted to be in the Peace Corps or that I wanted to demonstrate against nuclear arms, do you know how many of the kids would think I was just trying to be a saint?"

"In other words, trying to be good is bad, and being bad is good?"

"You got it."

Does the above conversation sound familiar? Does it make you angry? It does me. Here's what I hear being said:

1. You live in a world that doesn't seem to believe in saints anymore, or even in the desire to be one.
2. You live in a world that tends to love the person who is shrewd, clever, ambitious, "a real climber," a winner, but secretly mocks the person who wants to serve others, make sacrifices, fights for his or her beliefs, or is just a traditionally good person, good neighbor, and good family member.
3. You live in a world that often believes the lyrics to "Only the Good Die Young."
4. You are a fool if you believe you can make a dent in the massive problems of our world.
5. You are wise to realize that you should look out for yourself first and foremost.
6. You are a fool if you let those in need take advantage of your generosity.
7. You are wise if you let those in need pull themselves up by their bootstraps.
8. "Why bust your butt trying to solve one crisis when the next one is just around the corner?"
9. "Leave the crises of our world to the bleeding

hearts who are still dumb enough to think they can change things."

10. "The only thing you can change is yourself."

"Goodie two shoes"

What an awful attitude it is to believe that to be wise to the ways of the world is to stop caring. It makes me furious to know that if one of you partied all weekend, got totally wiped out, slept with someone, lied to your parents, and even got in trouble with the law, that few of your friends would bat an eye or even find it worthy of homeroom gossip. However, if you said you were going with your church youth group to visit some people at a nursing home, you might very well get stares that clearly say, "What a 'goodie two shoes!'" Isn't it sad that trying to be good makes one thought of as a prude, naive, a nerd, or a religious fanatic? Isn't it time that we who do believe in being good come out of the closet and proclaim that trying to be good only makes one wiser, happier, healthier, and more likely to live a long and satisfying life? I believe it is.

Yet there are some of you out there who really believe it isn't worth the effort to try and make a difference, and that being good doesn't really matter anymore. There are still others of you who not only agree with the above, but because of that attitude honestly feel life isn't worth living.

Yes, there are some of you who believe in being good, and in the necessity of goodness in making any real difference in your world, who are just worn out and worn down by the brand "goodie two shoes." I believe that some of the young people who have taken their own lives in this country have done so because it is bad to be good. It is a national tragedy that we have lost some of our best youth to the cynicism that says nobody can make a difference, and that "nice people finish last." Now maybe we can fully understand why Jesus said the first will be last, and the last first (Matt. 19:30). Maybe only Jesus can get us back to knowing that goodness matters in his eyes, and that making a difference is what being a disciple is all about. Let's turn now to Jesus to find out his response to the question, "Can I honestly hope to make a difference?"

Who would have ever thought?

The four of us had once been the starting backfield for our high school football team. We now looked like the fan club for the Pillsbury Doughboy. We had gathered together at Brusha's Pizza, a place where we had gone after every game. Fifteen years had passed, and at first the conversation was sort of awkward and slow. I was surprised when someone started telling stories about my father, and for the next two hours, the whole topic of discussion was my dad.

They told about my dad putting little bouquets of flowers out for us to take to our kindergarten teachers, the four of us having gone through all of our school years together. One reminisced about when my father had painted himself down our basement steps and into the corner by the coal bin. Being a stubborn man, he decided to wait it out. Being his shrewd son, I went around the block and sold tickets to see him. I made

$2.00! Another told about the time Dad took us fishing, and he parked his car on what appeared to be deserted railroad tracks. He said, "These tracks are all rusted—there hasn't been a train here in a century." After fishing, we found our car about three hundred yards down the tracks attached to a train. We still laugh at the stories, but what the boys remembered best was that my dad laughed, that he was always able to laugh at himself.

The trip down memory lane continued. They talked about how Dad had put water cups out for us during football season, so that we dry, dirty players could stop by for a drink at my house, since the practice field, over a mile from school, had none. They reminded me that Dad was the only father who always asked, "Did you have a good time?" after every football game, and never seemed to care how I did. He never pressured me. Most of all they talked about how Dad had so many funny stories to tell, and that he was always interested in them. He always asked them a million questions and he honestly listened to their answers.

I hate to admit this, but in high school I wasn't very proud of my dad. He didn't have a college education. He didn't have a prestigious job or a fancy car, and we didn't have much money. That night, at Brusha's Pizza, I realized that my father had made a huge difference in all of our lives by just being such a great dad. Who would have ever thought he would have dominated the conversation after 15 years? Who would have ever thought that our favorite memories would have been about someone that the world hardly noticed? Who would have ever thought my dad could have made such a difference? Well, he did, and you can too—maybe just by being able to laugh at yourself, being able to tell a good story, or being someone that other people love to be around.

Good soil can make a difference

> His disciples asked him what this parable meant. He said, "The knowledge of the secrets of the kingdom of God has been given to you, but to others I speak in parables, so that,
>
> " 'though seeing, they may not see;
> though hearing, they may not understand.'
>
> "This is the meaning of the parable: The seed is the word of God. Those along the path are the ones who hear, and then the devil comes and takes away the word from their hearts, so that they may not believe and be saved. Those on the rock are the ones who receive the word with joy when they hear it, but they have no root. They believe for a while, but in the time of testing they fall away. The seed that fell among thorns stands for those who hear, but as they go on their way they are choked by life's worries, riches and pleasures, and they do not mature. But the seed on good soil stands for those with a noble and good heart, who hear the word, retain it, and by persevering produce a crop."
>
> (Luke 8:9-15)

Like in the parable, there are those of you whose faith is shallow, a faith grown on rocky soil where the roots cannot go deep, and who enjoy your faith and your church until you are tested or some action is expected from you. Some people just like to admire

Jesus. They never expect to be called to follow him. Many of you are choked by constant worrying over the good life, the riches and pleasures of the world. There is just no room for Jesus, no time for goodness, and no energy left to worry much about being a disciple.

This passage, however, also tells us that good soil will bear fruit. A faith that is planted in good soil will make a difference; it will yield a rich harvest of goodness. What makes for good soil? Think about it:

1. *Watering*—feeding the soil with constant sources of strength, and that means prayer, worship, the study of Scripture, time alone with God, time to offer praise and thanksgiving, forgiving others and being forgiven, and living out the hope of a new you, a new you promised by your Baptism.
2. *Weeding*—getting rid of those attitudes and behaviors that still threaten to choke your faith to death, and that means avoiding any idolatry, from material things to sex to chemicals.
3. *Fertilizing*—making the soil even richer and more productive in the eyes of Christ, and that means serving others, making genuine sacrifices, and taking the risk of even loving your enemies.
4. *Harvesting*—trusting that good soil will yield good fruit and that it is important only to know when to harvest, and that means to know when to pray, when to pick up your crosses, and even when to love and to forgive.

Good soil can make a difference, since good soil can grow a strong, fertile faith, and we have been promised that faith can even move mountains.

> Jesus replied, "I tell you the truth, if you have faith and do not doubt, not only can you do what was done to the fig tree, but also you can say to this mountain, 'Go, throw yourself into the sea,' and it will be done. If you believe, you will receive whatever you ask for in prayer."
>
> (Matt. 21:21-22)

Real love can make a difference

The apostle Paul described for us all what *real love* is about in probably the most famous passage of Scripture in our culture:

> If I speak in the tongues of men and of angels, but have not love, I am only a resounding gong or a clanging cymbal. If I have the gift of prophecy and can fathom all mysteries and all knowledge, and if I have a faith that can move mountains, but have not love, I am nothing. If I give all I possess to the poor and surrender my body to the flames, but have not love, I gain nothing.
>
> Love is patient, love is kind. It does not envy, it does not boast, it is not proud. It is not rude, it is not self-seeking, it is not easily angered, it keeps no record of wrongs. Love does not delight in evil but rejoices with the truth. It always protects, always trusts, always hopes, always perseveres.
>
> Love never fails. But where there are prophecies, they will cease; where there are tongues, they will be stilled; where there is knowledge, it will pass away. For we know in part and we prophesy in part, but when perfection comes, the imperfect disappears. When I was a child, I talked like a child, I thought like a child, I reasoned like a child. When I became a man, I put childish ways behind me. Now we see but a poor

reflection; then we shall see face to face. Now I know in part; then I shall know fully, even as I am fully known.

And now these three remain: faith, hope, and love. But the greatest of these is love.

(1 Corinthians 13)

Unfortunately, even though this passage from l Corinthians is read at almost every wedding service from Burbank to Boston, few people seem to really hear Paul's message. The message is simply that *real love*, the kind that can make a real difference, requires real work. In a world that makes love sound as instinctual as eating or drinking, it is hard for us to be told that love is work, effort, or as Erich Fromm put it, "an art." We like to think of love as something that happens with effortless ease and not something that, as Paul suggests, requires great patience, a selfless nature, and avoiding the desire to pout or get even.

Although I can't prove it, I believe that most of you not only know what real love is, but also know what it takes to make it last. The divorce rate, I'm afraid, is not due to ignorance of the work required by love and marriage, but rather an arrogance in thinking one has already mastered the art. Most of you have a good idea of the kind of effort required by a real love, but you overestimate your readiness to take the exam. Each of you has the capacity to create a beautiful painting of real love. You may even already have in your head a vision of the landscape itself, or the portrait, the colors, the shadings, even the crucial perspective. However, few of you seem ready and willing to go through the grind of churning out a stack of sketches before you choose to apply the paint to the canvas. You would be wise to keep Fromm's image of an artist in your mind and heart when it comes to loving, because it will remind you of the labor involved in producing what looks like such a natural and effortless extension of your self. Real love requires work and work requires time, and a real love that has been given both real effort and a ton of time will make a difference.

Carolyn

Recently, my wife and I shared the very tough task of preaching at the funeral of our closest friends' 11-year-old daughter. We had decided to both give brief sermons, so that if either one of us fell apart, the other could fill in. The funeral, in fact the whole experience of Carolyn's death, was a strange mixture of grief, relief, and explosions of joy. Carolyn's life had always been tenuous, with a heart defect that troubled her from birth.

When I faced the congregation on the day of Carolyn's funeral, I knew there were two questions that haunted every person there: "How do we make any sense out of this?" and "Where do we go from here?" Both questions came out of the belief that Carolyn had been cheated out of so much, and so had her friends and her family. I was certain that the congregation who gathered to say good-bye to Carolyn was angry with God and had come not wanting to hear anything about a heaven they felt had become home to Carolyn much too early.

I preached then what I share with you now, and that is a look at Carolyn's life through the eyes of Jesus

Christ. By the world's standards Carolyn was cheated, because the world measures by amounts and accumulations. However, by Jesus' standards, which are always measured by quality and true value, Carolyn's life was complete and full and finished. Those of us who knew Carolyn well also knew that she was aware of what really mattered in life, for Carolyn in her brief time on earth had loved her neighbor as her self, and her God with her whole heart. Carolyn was the same little girl who gave a large portion of her birthday money to feed the hungry, who cried when my wife's children's sermon told about the black children of South Africa, who always came home from long, tough visits to the hospital telling of kids much worse off than she, who hid brownies for her favorite doctor, and who told her very tired mother many, many times, "We'll get through this." Carolyn was a fighter, a person who lived with great courage for one so young. Carolyn was so clearly a child of God, a little girl who in God's eyes had accomplished big things.

Carolyn proved that love can make a difference. She was full of love, love received from parents, her brother, her friends, her God, and love that was just a natural part of Carolyn. She gave love, she shared love, she inspired and ignited love, and she was love. Carolyn was more than just a cute, perky, 11-year-old, she was a person who just oozed love, and one could see in her face that she somehow knew what really mattered in life. Even before her death, I always found Carolyn to be so at peace with herself, her world, her life, and her well-known condition. Carolyn was not cheated, except maybe for time itself.

But as for what makes time worth experiencing—love—of that she had a ton.

Carolyn made a difference in so many lives, not by dying young, but by living bravely and beautifully. Carolyn will never be forgotten by those who loved her, for her love still warms our hearts and minds and memories. Where do we go from here? I think we go where Carolyn had gone, filling each day with all the love we can muster, making every moment count, and never ever feeling cheated by a God who loves Carolyn, and you, literally to pieces.

Real happiness can make a difference

> Now when he saw the crowds, he went up on a mountainside and sat down. His disciples came to him, and he began to teach them, saying:
>
> "Blessed are the poor in spirit,
> for theirs is the kingdom of heaven.
> Blessed are those who mourn,
> for they will be comforted.
> Blessed are the meek,
> for they will inherit the earth.
> Blessed are those who hunger and thirst for righteousness,
> for they will be filled.
> Blessed are the merciful,
> for they will be shown mercy.
> Blessed are the pure in heart,
> for they will see God.
> Blessed are the peacemakers,
> for they will be called sons of God.
> Blessed are those who are persecuted because of righteousness,
> for theirs is the kingdom of heaven.

> "Blessed are you when people insult you, persecute you and falsely say all kinds of evil against you because of me. Rejoice and be glad, because great is your reward in heaven, for in the same way they persecuted the prophets who were before you."
>
> (Matt. 5:1-12)

I have come to believe, again against popular opinion, that most of you understand Jesus' idea of happiness, and also his meaning in the Beatitudes. I have come to this conclusion by asking many of you about happiness, and noticing the tremendous difference there is in your answers when the question includes the word *real*. I admit that when I ask you what makes you happy I usually hear about a new outfit, a rock concert, or an upcoming vacation or dance. However, if I put an emphasis on the word *real*, "What makes you really, I mean down deep, really happy?" the answers often reflect a genuine faith, and even a genuine understanding of the Beatitudes.

Let me share with you some of the responses to that question of real happiness I have heard and recorded over the years from high school students:

- "I love tucking my little sister in bed. It just makes me feel terrific."
- "My social studies class adopted a South American child as a project, and I worked a lot on it, sort of in charge, I guess, and it made me feel so good inside."
- "When I talk with my girlfriend about serious stuff, personal things, I feel so close to her it hurts. I even get a pain in my chest."
- "Whenever I really pray, I mean not a table or

bedtime thing, but really pray, I feel so relaxed, so at peace."

- "I stood up for this one guy at school that everyone always teases, and I told the guys to knock it off. I felt proud of myself."
- "We had a dance for world hunger at school, and a hike for it at our church. At both events we sang 'We Are the World,' and the look on everyone's face really shook me up. You could tell how much everyone cared."
- "Walking in the woods alone. Everything is just so quiet, so beautiful. Awesome."
- "I really disappointed my parents big last year—I mean big time—and my dad came into my room one night and just told me that he loved me, and that it was over. I felt so relieved and so happy. We hugged for a long time."
- "My best friend at school lost her mom to cancer, and at the funeral almost the whole class showed up. I know it meant so much to her to have us there."
- "At youth group, when we prayed for peace and everyone held hands, I just wanted peace so bad. I mean no war, no war in my lifetime or in my kids'."

These are just a few responses I have recorded, but each reflects a deep appreciation of *real* happiness. Real happiness goes so much deeper than "good times," "good looking," or "the good life." It goes to the core of our faith, to being a good person. A good person brings out the best in others, sees the good in each person, and the beauty in life's smallest events.

A good person knows that true tears often show true happiness, and that we feel the deepest sense of happiness when we have worked hard, painfully hard, to get to that point. We feel happiest when we have taken the risk of trying to make a difference. I hope you will keep on taking that risk. You may not change the course of history or become an international hero, but you can become a hero in the eyes of Christ.

9

"CAN I BE FORGIVEN?"

All of you at some point probably have done something or said something or even thought something that you felt was so rotten, so sinful, so bad, even God could not forgive you. For most of you the feeling of being unforgiveable fades away in a day or two, and you get back to feeling sinful but forgiven again. However, for some this feeling of being unforgiveable haunts you. It may depart for a brief spell, but it always comes back to frighten you again.

What makes someone your age feel so unforgiveable, so haunted by the ghostly question, "Can I be forgiven?" Let me share with you some of the reasons and experiences that I've observed make some of you feel so distant from God, unworthy of God's grace.

Feeling responsible

Brad had told his sister he hated her and he wished she were dead. The following day she was killed in a car accident. Sheila had run away from home one summer, after a major argument with her father, and in late August her father had a fatal heart attack. Mike was certain that his poor academic performance and dabbling in drugs had created the stress that led to his parents splitting up, since they appeared to always be fighting over him. Margaret was the victim of incest, and she still believed that she must have done something to make her father act toward her the way that he did. Kerry was certain that his father's beatings were somehow deserved, and that there must be something evil about him to make his father so angry. Teresa felt that her mother hated her from the day she was born, because she was always being told that raising her had cost her mother all of her dreams.

These young persons saw themselves as responsible for the physical or emotional destruction of an individual or family, or for actually creating the sickness of which they were in fact the victim. All of these young people saw themselves as creators of evil, like the devil himself. When you think of yourself as the devil, or having the power to create evil, is it any wonder you would see yourself as unforgiveable?

It is hard to make Margaret realize that she is in no way responsible for her father's sexual advances. *The adult is always responsible, not the child.* It is difficult for Sheila to understand that her father's heart was defective and not destroyed by her. When so much emotion and often so much tragedy is involved, it is hard to keep things in perspective. Yet, it is critical for people to remember that they are not the devil, and they probably did not create the evil that torments them. This is not to say that one is not capable of an evil action or making a potentially evil choice. We are human beings, not God. We are human beings, not the devil. Human beings are always forgiveable.

Have you ever told a lie, a real whopper, and gotten somebody in big trouble? What if the lie cost someone their job or the love of their life or a really good friendship? Have you ever said something purposefully mean to another person, something really aimed at hurting them? What if after that the person became depressed or even suicidal? How would you feel? Words *can* do harm. What we say can be responsible for inflicting great pain on another human being or doing someone great harm. As a consequence, we may feel so responsible that we feel unforgiveable.

Even though we all have regretted our own words, and we've told a whopper or two or three, seldom did we ever really want tragedy to strike. We've all plotted revenge at some point in our lives, but I seriously doubt we ever wanted that revenge to become a genuine tragedy. We are human and at times are filled with hate, anger, rage, jealousy, and the desire to get even. However, most of the time those feelings are impulses of the moment. They seldom reflect a real plot to create a tragic situation.

Feeling dirty

Many young people who feel unforgiveable do so as the result of something sexual. I have heard this unforgiveability expressed in terms of being too "dirty" to be made clean. The following list includes some of the kinds of sexual behavior that have led some of you to feel unworthy of God's love:

- Excessive masturbation.
- Premarital sexual relations.
- Using a person for sexual gratification only.
- Frequent enjoyment of pornography.
- Sleeping around with several partners.
- Having an abortion.
- Homosexual fantasies or feelings or involvements.
- Being a prostitute.
- Fantasies that seem perverted or really dirty or kinky.
- Constantly lying about your sexual behavior.

Sexuality is a most confusing area, and I know it is hard for you to deal with the powerful feelings and needs created by human physical desire. I also know that many of you can identify with the above list, in fact, more of you than most adults would ever want to admit. I don't want to go through that list and rank them one to ten, with ten being the "dirtiest." We all have thought and felt dirty at some point sexually, as there is probably no more complex moral area in life. I'm not endorsing dirty thoughts or actions. Rather, I am just admitting that sex can let us feel the best and the worst in life, and because it is such a complex thing, people are bound to make some mistakes, at times serious ones. You must never make the mistakes your goal, but instead try to be honest about your sexual attitudes and behaviors and be willing to claim responsibility for them. Jesus only asks you to be honest sexually, to know in your heart and faith that you are acting responsibly and maturely and with love.

Since this is not a book on teenage sexuality, I won't even attempt to dive into all the moral and ethical choices that go along with that territory. Instead, I will stick to the issue at hand, forgiveness. Jesus does not rank sins, and sexual sins are also included in God's forgiveness. Since sex is one of God's most precious and enjoyable gifts, it is expected that you will treat it with respect and maybe even awe. If you are honest with yourself and with Jesus as to your sexual behavior, then I believe he will assist you in sexually becoming the responsible, loving adult you were created to be. There is nothing that is unforgiveable; the only requirement is the actual coming to the source of forgiveness, Jesus Christ. Feeling dirty is an awful experience, but the cleansing powers of Christ are *unlimited.*

I can't stop!

We humans foolishly pride ourselves on always being in control, thinking we can solve all of our own problems. Sometimes we are in control and do a great job in handling our problems, but at other times we run up against that one issue or problem we just can't seem to do much about. There are millions of Americans who have lost control of their lives to chemicals. Others—and there are a great many of them—can't stop making themselves throw up (bulimia) or get themselves to stop dieting (anorexia nervosa). Still more are addicted to nicotine, or food, or excitement to the point of self-destruction, and they just can't find the willpower to quit. All of these folks, which may include your parents, your neighbors, your friends, or you, are compulsive people, and they just don't seem able to stop what they are doing. In other words, the compulsion is in control. And a frequent side effect of feeling out of control is feeling unforgiveable.

The feeling of being unforgiveable is due to their fear and anger over having lost control. The person's life becomes littered with broken promises, broken spirits, and broken dreams. People who are compulsively out of control feel worthless, weak, foolish, and crazy, because otherwise there is no reason to explain their behavior. How could God forgive someone with no willpower? How could God forgive someone who can't beat even a little problem? The lousier these people feel about themselves, the more out of control they become, and the more unforgiveable they feel.

If you are out of control, compulsive in some area, you know how unforgiveable you often feel. You feel shame, embarrassment, and a terrific need to lie and cover up. You punish yourself by saying that even God has given up on you, or by continuing to tell yourself that you can quit anytime you really want to. Remember, the key to quitting, the key to regaining control, is not in your becoming stronger of will, but becoming stronger of faith, strong enough to turn the problem over to God. I would encourage you to attend an open AA (Alcoholic Anonymous) meeting sometime, even if you have no problem with alcohol, and see how turning the problem over to God is the key to recovery. Once you turn over a problem to God's power, you will also realize that God forgives. In fact, in taking your problem from you, God clearly says that you have already been forgiven.

If you feel you are involved in some behavior you know in your heart is destructive and you know you can't stop doing it, then come to Jesus and turn that compulsion over to him. Jesus will never turn anyone away. His forgiveness is available to all who seek it.

If you only knew!

During my ministry I have encountered some youths who felt unforgiveable because of criminal or satanic involvements in the past. When Chuck was 12 years old, he deliberately set several fires. One fire he started in a neighbor's garage destroyed numerous antiques with great sentimental value, all of which were being stored there for refinishing. Chuck came to see me at age 17, still consumed in guilt and still recalling clearly how his neighbor sobbed uncontrollably over the loss of her treasured possessions. Keith had gotten into Satan worship at age 14. His arms were permanently scarred with Satan-oriented tattoos, remnants of a past that involved terrorizing a neighborhood, especially an elderly man who Keith's group actually drove from his home. Keith was now 19, but he was still possessed by his own guilt for having done a great many destructive acts.

Both of these boys had come from very troubled homes. One boy had a violent, alcoholic parent, and the other's parents were engaged in verbally violent divorce proceedings. Both of these boys were involved in destructive behavior for a short time, mainly as a way of showing their own violent anger over family situations beyond their control. Both felt unforgiveable. Both believed the damage done was damage that could not be repaired. Both were right. Nothing could replace those antiques, and nothing could repair the damage done to an old man who was frightened out of his home of 57 years.

Jesus does not magically make the hurt and pain caused by these two boys somehow disappear. What he can do is remind them that the destruction must stop and that feeling endless guilt does not serve him. Endless guilt serves no one. Jesus can only promise Chuck and Keith the fullness of forgiveness and the hope that they will make up for the damage done by living lives dedicated to the love of neighbor and God. Both young men are doing just that, and both are beginning to feel the cleansing of God's forgiving love. Both young men came to me saying, "If you only knew." Eventually I did know, but more importantly Chuck and Keith realized that Jesus knew, and had always known, and had always offered his forgiveness. It was just that now they were ready to receive it.

What a waste!

One final group of young people that I have observed as feeling unforgiveable are those who have wasted an unbelievable amount of time or talent. Some have wasted their opportunities to get a good education or to learn as much as possible with the talented brains God gave them. Some have wasted their athletic or artistic abilities in order to conform to a group. Some have wasted precious time that could have been spent with family or friends, choosing instead to spend time getting into trouble. Some of you have already wasted a lot of years being somebody you are not. Some have lost those years to chemicals. Yes, some of you feel unforgiveable because you have wasted so much for so long, and so much of it can never be recaptured.

No, you are not unforgiveable. Part of the promise of the grace of God is that it is never too late, that we can always start fresh, and we can make up for time wasted yesterday by spending time wisely today. If you feel your past is pretty empty, fill up your present with a life of love and learning and using all the gifts you too have been given.

Maybe you can't really identify with feeling unforgiveable. You may even be more than a bit shocked to find out that so many teenagers have such heavy-duty problems. However, there are some of you who really struggle with the issue of sin and who have in fact come to the conclusion that you are "lost" in the eyes of God. At times Christian books for adolescents, like this one, have been written in a style that makes it clear they are intended for the untroubled, unbothered, and unaware young person, and as I have heard from so many of you, they barely even touch the real issues of being a teenager in today's world. I have written this book for both the troubled teen who needs some honest emotional and spiritual guidance and for the untroubled teen who is in an excellent position to be of genuine assistance to those friends who are hurting. So, even if the issue of forgiveness has never been a big one for you, I hope you will use the following information as a way of learning how to help someone else deal with being forgiven.

Sinners identified

I have always used a simple, working definition of *sin,* and that is that sin is "being unloving." The dictionary definition of *sin* is "missing the mark"—not measuring up to God's standards for us. And Jesus said that the most important thing God expects from us is to love God and love our neighbor (Matt. 22:37-39). Anytime we are unloving to self, to someone else, to God, even to God's creation, then we are probably sinning. I have also always had what I think is a fairly simple and accurate definition of *sinner,* and that is "anyone who is alive." We are all sinners, and whenever I confess my own sins I am amazed at how "unloving" I can be, especially to my self. The fact that we are all sinners and we are all in need of Christ's cleansing powers is well stated in the following scripture passage:

> If we claim to be without sin, we deceive ourselves and the truth is not in us. If we confess our sins, he is faithful and just and will forgive us our sins and purify us from all unrighteousness. If we claim we have not sinned, we make him out to be a liar and his word has no place in our lives.
>
> (1 John 1:8-10)

This passage goes right to the heart of the matter: sin is just inevitable. You know you sin. I know I sin. We all know we sin. God certainly knows we sin. So, why bother covering up?

Those of you who feel unforgiveable need to see that being a sinner is not the same as being evil, but it is the same as being human. You are not evil, you are sinful and human, and those two are pretty well glued together. If you are feeling unforgiveable, it is simply best to confess your sin to God, to get that "infection" out of your system. If you bring that sin to Jesus, there is no question of your acceptability for grace. Jesus doesn't rank sin or sinners; he promises to forgive all those who empty their sin into the bottomless well of his love and mercy.

No such thing as unforgiveable

Jesus continued: "There was a man who had two sons. The younger one said to his father, 'Father, give me my share of the estate.' So he divided his property between them.

"Not long after that, the younger son got together all he had, set off for a distant country and there squandered his wealth in wild living. After he had spent everything, there was a severe famine in that whole country, and he began to be in need. So he went and hired himself out to a citizen of that country, who sent him to his fields to feed pigs. He longed to fill his stomach with the pods that the pigs were eating, but no one gave him anything.

"When he came to his senses, he said, 'How many of my father's hired men have food to spare, and here I am starving to death! I will set out and go back to my father and say to him: Father, I have sinned against heaven and against you. I am no longer worthy to be called your son; make me like one of your hired men.' So he got up and went to his father.

"But while he was still a long way off, his father saw

> him and was filled with compassion for him; he ran to his son, threw his arms around him and kissed him.
>
> "The son said to him, 'Father, I have sinned against heaven and against you. I am no longer worthy to be called your son.'
>
> "But the father said to his servants, 'Quick! Bring the best robe and put it on him. Put a ring on his finger and sandals on his feet. Bring the fattened calf and kill it. Let's have a feast and celebrate. For this son of mine was dead and is alive again; he was lost and is found.' So they began to celebrate."
>
> (Luke 15:11-24)

I love the parable of the prodigal son for so many reasons, but mainly because it is such an accurate description of most human relationships with God. The human being in the story, in typical fashion, wants to get his piece of the good life, and he wants to have it without any interference from his overprotective parent. Just like God, the father in the story gives his very human son full freedom to go off and fall flat on his arrogant face. The human being, good old prodigal son, does just that, and goes off and blows just about everything, including losing most of what Dad had given him as his personal treasure. While feasting on "Pig Chow Helper" the human gets a bright idea: he would be happier under the care of his dad. Totally empty-handed, the complete fool, feeling *unforgiveable,* the son comes home to his father, and the father embraces him with a squeeze that could turn a bushel of oranges into pure juice in about a split second. The human son can't believe his stupidity is forgiven. The father can't believe it took his son "Pig Chow Helper" to see the light.

If you are feeling unforgiveable, isn't it time for you to come home to God? If you feel like you've made a complete mess of your life, isn't it time for you to get out of the swamp and into the clean living of being home with Jesus? Could you have possibly screwed up any worse than the prodigal son? I really doubt it.

Guilt garbage

The prodigal son was probably stunned to be so fully and joyfully forgiven, and he probably wondered why he wasn't sent to his room to feel guilty for a decade. I think God knew he had felt enough guilt and that any more guilt would just be garbage. It is better to turn the garbage into fertilizer and grow something with it than to just drown in a quicksand of waste. If you are still feeling that God can't forgive you or that you haven't felt guilty long enough or deeply enough to justify being forgiven, ask yourself the following questions:

1. What good is your guilt doing you, anyone else, or God?
2. How much guilt is enough?
3. How long should a person feel guilty?
4. Is it easier to be guilty or to pick up your cross and follow Jesus?
5. Is it easier to see yourself as unforgiveable or to get on with being a disciple dedicated to the art of caring?
6. What talents, gifts, and acts of discipleship have been wasted while you've marched in place feeling guilty?

7. Is God's power limited? Is that why you can't be forgiven?
8. Is the possibility of becoming a totally new person in Jesus Christ really frightening you?

Guilt is good if it produces confession. Guilt is bad if it just piles up like garbage and continues to stink up your life and leaves you swarming with feelings of being unforgiveable. Don't waste one more minute of your life, of your God-given self, feeling you can't change, you can't become a better person, you can't be forgiven. Get on with it: learn to live, to love, to be a disciple. Pick up the cross of your guilt and follow Christ, and soon you will be strong enough to tell someone else who feels just like you, "You, too, are forgiven."

10
"CAN ANYTHING MAKE THE PAIN GO AWAY?"

The underlying theme of this book has been that adolescence is often a time filled with many painful questions. Not all of you are troubled or in trouble, nor are all of your lives consumed in a painful quest for answers. Still, more and more of you are grappling with these issues, and almost all of you will be touched by someone who is facing questions that might even threaten their lives. Remember, it is tough enough to grow up as it is, and for those of you who are battling some of the issues raised in this book, it can be overwhelming at times. I think it would be helpful to review here the kinds of questions I hear more and more of you asking, and the kinds of pain the questions reflect:

1. "Why me?"—*the pain of feeling rage.*
2. "Will anything ever be the same again?"—*the pain of feeling grief.*

3. "Will I ever be somebody really special?"—*the pain of feeling anonymous.*
4. "How many happy adults do you know?"—*the pain of feeling hopeless.*
5. "Is life just an endurance test that nobody ever passes?"—*the pain of feeling bored.*
6. "What's the big deal about suicide, if I feel dead already?"—*the pain of feeling hollow.*
7. "Will there be a world to live in when I'm 30?"—*the pain of feeling terror.*
8. "Can I honestly hope to make a difference?"—*the pain of feeling insignificant.*
9. "Can I be forgiven?"—*the pain of feeling guilt.*
10. "Can anything make the pain go away?"—*the pain of feeling anxious.*

These questions are real. These pains are real. There are many of you who understand the experience of both. The pain and the questioning going on in many of your lives are real, and we cannot pretend they do not exist. Even Jesus Christ can do nothing about that which you won't claim, or the world won't claim as *real.*

Overwhelmed

One day after church I asked Julia how she was doing. She replied, "I'm feeling pretty out of it—sort of overwhelmed, if you know what I mean." I asked her to come in to talk some day after school, and she did. As it turned out, Julia had good reason to feel overwhelmed.

Julia was having a terrible spring. She and her boyfriend had decided to break up before college, so that they could date other people. Julia's grandfather had died in April, and he had always been very special to her. Her SAT scores were not as good as she had hoped, and she was still awaiting word on whether the college of her choice had accepted her. Everyone kept asking her where she was going to college and what she was going to study there, and she had no answer to either question. She had put on 15 pounds in the past two months and had no date for the Prom. She was secretly frightened of graduating and leaving home, and she was finding herself drinking more than usual. Everywhere she went she felt like it might be for the last time, and so she was always feeling a bit sad. She had a small accident with her parent's car in May. She came down with mono the first week in June.

As Julia summed it all up, "I just feel like I'm drowning, and I have so many questions about everything. What do I want to do? Will I make it in college? Why did I break up with Bo? Why can't I lose weight? Should I ask Frank to Prom? I'm worried about my drinking. I'm sad all the time. I just feel rotten, and I can't stop worrying."

When you feel overwhelmed with questions, you may also find yourself seeking to *escape.* There is not much wrong with escaping once in a while, but you need to be careful that you don't find yourself constantly running away from your problems. Remember, the need to escape can be *addictive.* Some of you may even find yourselves doing things to escape that you know are dangerous, or even life threatening. It's not uncommon for people who feel overwhelmed and seek to escape to do so with chemicals (as Julia was starting to do). It is also not uncommon for people your age to escape by losing themselves in the crowd. Even escaping to one's room or into one's music is potentially dangerous if it produces an isolation from others and from the world. Constant escaping is always damaging, sometimes physically, sometimes emotionally or relationally, and always spiritually.

The final escape for some of you is thinking about suicide, and for many suicidal youth the goal is not death, but simply an escape from the *pain of life*. Kids who have entertained the notion of suicide have expressed their thoughts to me in these terms:

"I wanted to kill myself for a little while."

"I don't want to die, I just don't want to live like this anymore."

"I need a break, a long break. I am so tired, I could sleep forever."

"I just ran out of tough."

"I want everything to stop, just for a while."

What you have to remember, and what suicidal youth try to ignore, is that suicide is a *final* solution to a *temporary* problem.

Becoming volcanos

I got tired just watching Justin. He was jammed with energy, and he was always positive and upbeat. In fact, I began to notice that he was honestly too "up." He was always on the go, attending every party, serving on every school project or committee, studying, dating a dozen different girls, and always jogging. He was like a person possessed. He never slowed down, he never stopped smiling, and he never stopped talking, even though it was usually about nothing.

At a certain point I could tell that Justin was about ready to explode. He often got angry and always seemed irritable. He was tired looking and getting thin. He hardly ever ate or slept, and he could not sit still. He kept running, farther and farther every day. He began to complain of headaches and nausea, and he always seemed to have a cold. He was falling behind in school, and he wasn't following through on his responsibilities at home, school, youth group, or the many committees he was on.

One day Justin bounced into my office, acting once again like he was Mr. Happy-Go-Lucky. I put my hands on his shoulders and said to him, "Justin, cut the act, you're like a walking volcano, and you're going to erupt." Erupt he did, into torrents of sobs. Justin, as I was soon to discover, was a very unhappy and frightened young man. He had little confidence in himself.

Unfortunately, like Justin, most of us have been taught to never admit our pain or claim our questions or searching. We have been told to hold it in, to be strong, and to get our acts together. Many of you have pushed these questions so far down that they have become like molten lava in the center of your self. You have denied your feelings, ignored your questions, avoided your pain, and now on some days you feel about ready to explode. You are convinced that your friends would either laugh or not understand, your parents would lecture, and seeing a counselor would brand you as crazy, so you keep on holding it all in.

In a very real way you, too, have become a walking volcano.

As volcanos are prone to do, once in awhile there are spurts of lava that flow down the sides for a brief spell. You might experience such spurts as the following:

1. Being extremely irritable, especially with parents, about almost everything.
2. Throwing a real temper tantrum.
3. Picking on someone at school, or making one person your scapegoat or personal dumping ground.
4. Finding yourself physically violent at times, expressing the need to punch something or break something.
5. Saying exceptionally cruel things you know you don't mean.
6. Finding your fantasies filled with plots of revenge or getting even.
7. Thinking about writing a suicide note, the ultimate way to get even.
8. Suicidal fantasies.

Though some of you will never think about suicide as an option, some of you find these thoughts spurting forth uncontrollably, as the volcano of feelings explodes. Explosions are unpredictable. Explosions are messy. Explosions often hurt innocent victims. Explosions can even make you an innocent victim. One thing we do know, few volcanos never erupt. As long as you choose to live like a volcano, you never know when or how you will experience a potentially deadly eruption.

The key to avoiding these volcanic explosions is to learn how not to live as a walking volcano. There are no secure lids for a volcano; it is simply smarter to dismantle this mountain of denial. Here are some basic spiritual steps to removing the volcano:

1. Be honest with your self about your true feelings.
2. Claim your questions, no matter how painful.
3. Share your feelings carefully with those people you trust. (By carefully, I mean not all at once and only when you feel the other person is really able to listen.)
4. Raise your questions with adults you respect and trust.
5. If there is no one you trust or respect all that much, turn to someone you feel has proven to be trustworthy and worthy of respect from others.
6. Don't be afraid to cry.
7. Don't be afraid to be angry.
8. Don't be afraid to be afraid.
9. Share your feelings and fears and questions with Jesus. Pray!
10. Trust Jesus to remove the burden of your pain.

These 10 steps are simple, easy reminders to accept your self as a human being, to admit your weakness to others and to Jesus, and to know that he will give you the courage and strength you need. The volcano erodes whenever we feel it is OK to be human, but it grows more explosive every time we deny our humanness. The volcano is built on playing God, trying to look like the perfect robot, and being willing to claim our human feelings and questions.

Spirit strength

> "All this I have spoken while still with you. But the Counselor, the Holy Spirit, whom the Father will send in my name, will teach you all things and will remind you of everything I have said to you. Peace I leave with you; my peace I give you. I do not give to you as the world gives. Do not let your hearts be troubled and do not be afraid."
>
> (John 14:25-27)

The question, "Can anything make the pain go away?" can be answered in faith, "Yes, the Holy Spirit can make the pain go away." The Holy Spirit doesn't make the pain go away by removing our questions or by magically making the pain disappear. The Spirit gives us the strength, the courage, and the faith needed to face our questions and handle our pain. The Spirit, unlike the world, does not encourage us to deny our hurt or anger, to avoid grappling with life's tough issues, or to ignore the stress of life. The Holy Spirit teaches us to:

- know that life is stressful;
- know that being human is at times very painful;
- know that everyone has crosses to carry;
- accept the help of Jesus Christ;
- find in faith the internal strength needed to pick up our crosses;
- find in faith the remover of pain, which is the courage to trust Jesus;
- know there are no easy answers, just spiritually strong people who can live with tough questions;

- know that Jesus is the source of peace we seek, a peace that eases all pain.

The peace we seek is not to have a world without questions, a life without pain. Rather, it is a peace that comes from knowing we have the strength spiritually to handle whatever life dishes out. The peace provided by the Holy Spirit reduces pain by increasing our faith, our hope, our love. The peace provided by the Holy Spirit reduces pain by increasing our dependence on Jesus and increasing our willingness to serve him.

> For I am convinced that neither death nor life, neither angels nor demons, neither the present nor the future, nor any powers, neither height nor depth, nor anything else in all creation, will be able to separate us from the love of God that is in Christ Jesus our Lord.
> (Rom. 8:38-39)

You are never alone. You are never without Jesus. Nothing, not even life's toughest questions, not even life's greatest pains can separate you from the love of Jesus. Jesus loves you. He cares about your questions and your pains. He can help. Jesus can be a life-saving answer, if you will only bring your questions to him. There is not a question, a pain, an issue that Jesus does not understand or for which he cannot offer you help and guidance. Jesus is always there, always ready, always willing to help you find the answers, to help you find the spiritual strength, and to help you embrace and enjoy life to the fullest.